RISE UP

A Call to Leadership
for African American Women

Sylvia Rose

IVP

InterVarsity Press
Downers Grove, Illinois

InterVarsity Press
P.O. Box 1400, Downers Grove, IL 60515-1426
World Wide Web: www.ivpress.com
E-mail: mail@ivpress.com

InterVarsity Press® is the book-publishing division of InterVarsity Christian Fellowship/USA®, a student movement active on campus at hundreds of universities, colleges and schools of nursing in the United States of America, and a member movement of the International Fellowship of Evangelical Students. For information about local and regional activities, write Public Relations Dept., InterVarsity Christian Fellowship/USA, 6400 Schroeder Rd., P.O. Box 7895, Madison, WI 53707-7895, or visit the IVCF website at <www.ivcf.org>.

All Scripture quotations, unless otherwise indicated, are taken from the Holy Bible, King James Version.

Design: Cindy Kiple

Images: black woman standing: Jana Leon/Photonica
spine art (black woman): Ron Krisel/Getty Images

ISBN 0-8308-3212-2

Printed in the United States of America ∞

Library of Congress Cataloging-in-Publication Data

Rose, Sylvia, 1953-
  Rise up: a call to leadership for African American women / Sylvia
Rose.
    p. cm.
  Includes bibliographical references.
  ISBN 0-8308-3212-2 (pbk.: alk. paper)
  1. Leadership—Religious aspects—Christianity. 2. African American
women. 3. Vocation. I. Title.
  BV4597.53.L43R67 2004
  248.8'43'08996073—dc2

                                                                                        2004004357

P	18	17	16	15	14	13	12	11	10	9	8	7	6	5	4	3	2	1
Y	17	16	15	14	13	12	11	10	09	08	07	06	05	04				

To Tuesdays

CONTENTS

ACKNOWLEDGMENTS

To the memory of my brother Jimmy Ray Rose, whose spirit lifted the lives and eyes of all who knew him. Though a big man, he was completely transparent, and one could always see God in and through him.

To my ten remaining sisters and brothers, who have so patiently given me space and time to become what I believed I could.

To the women of Breakfast And A Word and the staff of Great Heritage Ministries: Thank you for your support, which came early and with consistency. My faith in you and what you can do has been exceeded only by your belief in me.

To Patricia Brown, Donna Davis, Maria Jones, Pam Parker, Mildred Steward and Pat Wiley: You have always seen more in me than I could, but your faith has elevated my sight.

INTRODUCTION
A Cry for Leadership

$\mathcal{T}$he state of the world today has released us of our option to sit and defer leadership to only men and a few women. Women are needed as never before. Myles Munroe says, "Your existence is evidence that this generation needs something that your life contains."[1] In essence, our calling has come from our mere existence on earth. You don't need to ask others why they think you are here and what they think you need to do. When you look into the mirror, that should be enough reminder that you are here for a purpose and called to do something for the world. It is tragic that we wait until we are called by individuals instead of heeding the call of the world. There are thousands who are just crying for someone to tell them who they can be. They run to prophets, preachers and psychics in earnest desire of a word that will bring clarity to what God has already said to them through creation.

The world needs women to stand in leadership, but black women in particular. We need to lead from the insight that we have had at the bottom. We need to take our valley experiences to those on the mountaintop. We need to serve as lawyers for those who, through mere birth and bad breaks, cannot know justice in a system that too often recognizes and rewards wealth. We must be jurists because we have been misjudged. We must sit on corporate boards and become CEOs because we work in a great majority of the blue-collar jobs that fill the coffers of the corporate world. We have been great mothers, but it's time for us to birth other things. This generation needs something that our lives contain, and we must answer their call.

THE CALL OF VACANCY AND NEED

When we fail to answer the call to leadership, often someone else will. But they will be unable to bring to the need what we have to offer. There are politicians that run unopposed, not because they are the best individuals for the job, but because some of us will not answer our call. There are pulpits that are vacant because we are caught up in political battles about our worthiness and our place, and we do not answer our call. Our judicial system is far too white and male dominated because we are not answering our call. We have decided too often to do what is easier and what our finances dictate. And we do it for years before we are honest enough to admit that we are unfulfilled and emotionally starved. Our calling is tied to our created purpose, and the world needs us to answer the call.

It must be noted that there is great sacrifice in choosing to answer your call. The world can and does turn with contemptible fervor on the very ones from which it seeks help. On a daily, consistent basis, it will bite the hand that feeds it, and it is indiscriminate about doing so. But we must answer the call upon our lives anyway. Someone has said,

People are unreasonable, illogical and self-centered, but you must love them anyway.

If you do good, people will accuse you of having selfish and ulterior motives, but you must do good anyway.

The good you do today will be forgotten by tomorrow, but you must do good anyway.

People favor underdogs, but they follow only top dogs. Go out and fight for some underdogs anyway.

The biggest ideas by the biggest minds can be shot down by the smallest people with the smallest minds, but you must think big anyway.

What you spend years building can be destroyed overnight, but you must build anyway.

Give the world the best you've got and you might get kicked in the teeth. But you must give the world the best you've got . . . anyway!

And you must do so because you can. The need that you were created to fill is calling you, and you must come from beneath the covers of comfort and heed the call.

CALLED FOR SUCH A TIME AS THIS

Esther was positioned in the king's house, safe from the harm that was being deviously planned for the Jews who stood without. She could have chosen to hide behind the promise of her position as future queen, but her uncle reminded her of ties to the pain of the present. There was a generation that needed something from her, and he told her that she had been called for such a time as that. The realization of her calling forced her to risk her life to be and do what she had been called through creation and design to be and do (see Esther 4:13-16).

Your community needs you, black woman, to return its moral compass to an upright position. Your home needs you, black woman, in absence of the men that have been lost through death, divorce and desertion. Your church needs you, black woman, for there are far too few men who worship and even fewer who will do the work. Your government needs you, black woman, to help make laws that are fair and just to more than just a few. Your schools need you, black woman, to teach our children who too often are lost in a system that does not reflect their culture in testing and that dismisses them as ineducable, untrainable and thereby useless to society. Your cities need

you, black woman, to hold positions of authority so that you can ensure the equitable dispersion of funds to the proper places. Your
neighborhood needs you, black woman, to restore the sanctity and
security that has been lost to the underworld of drugs and thugs.

For too long we have tried to hide safely in the falsehood of our
being the weaker sex, desiring to be covered and protected by men.
But through choice or chance our men are not present and we are not
covered; neither are we safe. There is a clarion call for black women
to heed in such a time as this. Martin Luther King Jr. said, "The urgency of the hour calls for leaders of wise judgment and sound integrity—leaders not in love with money, but in love with justice; leaders
not in love with publicity, but in love with humanity; leaders who can
subject their particular egos to the greatness of the cause."[2] The time
has come for us to see the greatness of the need, hear the call, fill the
void and lead.

1 BEING CHOSEN

Stand up to the naysayers who question your place.

$\mathcal{I}$ wonder what was wrong with Jesse's other boys. Tall and good-looking, strong and sturdy, it appeared any one of them could have easily adjusted to the role of king. Their daddy hoped so. Samuel thought so. But God said no. It seems to me it would have been better to pick a man who didn't stutter as your spokesman as he stood toe to toe with a pharaoh, one who had confidence and presence as a leader and not one who would ask to have his brother tag along. And I don't know if I will ever understand the choice of Gideon, who had to require not one, but two signs from God before he would believe what he was hearing. And why an old man, half dead, whose wife couldn't help but laugh at the thought that they would birth a new generation? Why a young peasant girl, too poor to have the education and trappings expected for one who would give birth to the King? When God knows the end from the beginning, why would he choose a young shepherd boy and crown him king, knowing that he would abuse his power, lean to his lust and murder a man of valor? Who can understand the mind of God, but God? Were these really God's choices, his *first* choices?

The choices of God have never been to the liking or understanding of man. It is in the selection of those who would lead his people that God sets himself above us most. Who can understand God? The truth is, we have a better chance of grasping God in things that he created or things that he has done than in the way he acts toward

people. Although we marvel at the universe, it tends to make sense
to us. There is a constant rotation of the sun and earth bringing about
sunrises and sunsets and seasons that we have found predictable. We
can portend when storms will come or when major shifts will occur
in the earth. But when it comes to God's relationship to his highest
creation, humanity, we are prone to pause and shake our head in dis-
belief, questioning, as did the psalmist who asked, "What is man that
you are mindful of him, the son of man that you care for him?"
(Psalm 8:4 NIV). God's love for us is beyond human understanding
and is demonstrated in the mercy that he extends to us daily. We saw
it at Calvary, and we have come to believe and accept this magnificent
act because it represents the basic tenets of our Christian faith. We
have somehow found that believable. But it is God's continual acts on
our behalf that seem to puzzle us most and leave us struggling to
make sense of it, that it might be palatable to us. For we see his love
and his mercy most in his choices of people.

In looking at the Word of God and the examples that we have
there, one thing is clear: God chooses whom he desires to do whatever he wants them to do. He never uses logic that we can understand. And we are no match to his intelligence. Paul stated that "the
foolishness of God is wiser than man's wisdom" (1 Corinthians 1:25
NIV). God doesn't play into our comfort zones. He makes his choice
and that's it. And although we may look at his choice and utter, "I
wonder why," we can never say that it was a bad one, because God
does not make mistakes.

I find it also interesting that he chose to let us see the full story
about those he chose. He could have withheld from his holy text the
part when Moses killed a man and ran. We didn't have to know about
David and his plot to steal Uriah's wife. Had God omitted the details
about his leaders, which showed their weaknesses, sins and frailties,

then the confusion that we have about his choices would not exist. But something worse would have happened. We would then have measured ourselves against a perceived perfection and concluded, as do far too many, that God could not possibly choose us.

WHY NOT YOU?

In the manner of so many whom God has chosen, one of the most difficult things for us to simply realize is that we are the ones he wants to use. Why would he choose us African American women, you might ask. Why would he *not* choose us? For every reason that can be listed as to why we would not be the ones chosen by God, there are reasons as to why we would be. In typical religious settings, the thought is that God chooses to use men first and then women. And it is the belief of some that the choice is never women.

In 1985 God used me as a vessel to infuse new music into my church: I composed a small hymnal of songs to specifically suit the worship needs of its people. I had been born into and raised as a member of this denomination and loved it dearly. In my travels throughout the country in my position with a college, I had studied the musical preferences of this church. Years after leaving that position I quietly worked on this project without letting anyone know what I was doing. I remember the day I told my husband that I had something in me that simply had to come out and that I needed to stop teaching and devote myself to it full time until I brought it to fruition. For fear of the discouragement that I felt would certainly come to me, I told no one else about it.

Once the hymnal was completed, it became something that African American churches, in particular, embraced on a widespread level throughout the country. But whereas the music was met with open arms, the vessel through which it had come was not. At a national conference, I was approached by a man who held up one of my books and startled me with the question, "Who do you think you are and what made you think that you should do something like this?" I stammered until I spit out the worst answer I could give to him: "I was just a vessel . . . being used . . . by God." He tossed the book on a table and said, "God doesn't use women!"

If it were up to people, we would dictate to God who he could and should not choose. We would probably list parameters wherein he would stay and specify what we consider to be fitting. Such a list would no doubt include male, white, upper-class, educated, professional, influential; for surely God should select people in the way we select our president, the most powerful person in the world. We would consider what is popular to Western civilization, because in our limited thinking, it has been so ingrained in us to believe that our culture and customs are somehow holy and must be special to God because they mean something to us.

Women must stop looking at God through the eyes of our history with men and realize that what he says about us and to us in his Word is not the same as what is said about us from many of our pulpits and in our religious books and journals.

He chooses to use us for the same reason he has chosen so many others in the past: we are willing vessels.

DON'T CAST YOUR FACE TO THE GROUND

For us to really deal honestly with the problem of our thinking that we are not chosen of God for positions of leadership, we must address the issue of our self-esteem. We cannot lose sight of the fact that we have had a history of abuse, subjugation and second-class citizenship, and it has impacted our psyche. All too often our response to this damaged psyche has been to consume items that are designed to make us appear as if we are doing far better emotionally and psychologically than we are.

African Americans account for a large percentage of retail sales, disproportionate to our numbers as a percentage of the U.S. population, spending nearly 20 billion dollars in clothing and purchasing cars at twelve times the rate of other Americans.[1] In far too many instances, our cars cost more than our homes. And *Black Enterprise* reported that African American women spend 61 percent more than white women on clothing, hair and manicures. A survey by Cotton Incorporated Lifestyle Monitor found that 46 percent of black women ages twenty-five to thirty-five are more apt to try new styles, compared to 28 percent of white women. Sixty-three percent of us believe that it is important to keep our wardrobe updated, with 41 percent choosing to sacrifice comfort for fashion.[2]

It is this inordinate focus on outer appearance that led Tarajee Maynor, a twenty-five-year-old mother of two, to leave her children locked inside a hot car as the temperature reached eighty-eight degrees, while she spent nearly four hours in an upscale hair salon, trying on clothes, getting her hair done and having a massage. Never once during that time did she consider going back to the car to check on her children, who had succumbed to the suffocating heat.[3]

This example of self-indulgence and misplaced priorities may be the extreme illustration of my point, but it is extreme only because it involves the actual death of children. For in many ways we too have brought death into our homes as a result of our poor judgment in deciding how we will spend money. We have all too often killed the hopes for our children's college funding when we have chosen instead to make sure they and ourselves wore the top designer clothing and had the greatest, latest fads. We have chosen exotic hairstyles, manicures and fine clothing over other necessities in life for years, and it must be considered a weak and improper response to our low self-esteem and our desire to feel good about who we are.

After the sudden death of a first-grade teacher, I was asked to finish the school year in her stead and was sorely disappointed to see the seven-year-old girls with hair extensions that gave them designs that were far too mature for them and boys with pierced ears and diamond studs. Our misplaced priorities in spending are giving the wrong message to our children, thus ensuring that yet another generation will struggle with the consequences of improper choices. In our spending choices we have made every effort to ensure that we are chosen of men and have lost sight of the fact that we are chosen of God.

THE BOARD ROOM NEEDS YOU

Our low self-esteem is also seen in the fact that we have bought into the beliefs that there are certain places we cannot go and things we should not do. The majority of Americans (women included) still believe that we are not quite ready for a woman to be president. It doesn't matter how qualified she may be; it is merely her gender that limits her. And in spite of the fact that former prime minister Margaret Thatcher, who led Britain for over a decade, was highly regarded on an international level, most Americans believe that running *our* country is not a job for a woman to do. We simply do not look at ourselves as measuring up, and we must reeducate ourselves and others to the reality of what we were created for and what we are capable of doing.

This reeducation must start at the right place. Simply recounting historical events and demonstrating our resilience and ability to overcome the obstacles before us may bring us a good feeling, but it may not altogether break the inferior thinking and mental bondage. The successful struggles of the suffrage and women's rights movements may provide inspiration to us. The vivid pictures of the civil rights movement and the fight for affirmative action may motivate and spur some of us to action. But there is not enough in any of those to remove some of the deep scars in our thinking and transform us into what we should be. We must go beyond and deeper than the roots of American history or feminism and reach for the only thing that truly liberates our minds: the love of God.

HE HAS SET HIS LOVE UPON US

Moses was always reminding the children of Israel of their covenant relationship with God. This reminder often rehearsed the many mighty and wonderful things that the Lord had done on their behalf. He told them that they were a holy, chosen and special people to the Lord, above all the people on the face of the earth. But Moses tried to let them see that God did not choose them for reasons that they may have felt. He said, "The LORD did not set his love upon you, nor choose you, because ye were more in number than any people; for ye were the fewest of all people: But because the LORD loved you, and because he would keep the oath which he had sworn unto your fathers" (Deuteronomy 7:6-7). I am convinced that few people, and women in particular, have been able to accept the fact that God loves them dearly, completely and without exception. His love is not because we are women. It is not in spite of our being African American women. It is simply because we are his creation and he delights in us. He loves us because he is God and he is love.

I listened recently to a woman talk of a series of horrible events that were taking place at her church because of abusive leadership. She began to cry. I looked her in her eyes and told her that the reason she and the other members felt they should submit themselves to such treatment was because they have never been convinced of how much God loves them. Their self-esteem allowed them only to see their pastor as being better than they, holier than they and closer to God than they, and thus they felt the treatment was justified even though they could recount no action on their part that would precipitate the abuse. I suggested that she search the Word of God to see just what he felt about her.

As long as we continue to look only at each other and ourselves, we will always fall short. We will also never understand, and will find it difficult to accept, the fullness of God's love. It will not make sense. It *does not* make sense. God has set his love upon us because he is a God of love. It's just that simple.

Samuel also wondered what was wrong with Jesse's older boys, until God told him the basis on which he makes his choice: "The LORD does not look at the things man looks at. Man looks at the outward appearance, but the LORD looks at the heart" (1 Samuel 16:7 NIV). If we have a heart toward God and we prepare ourselves to be willing vessels, we will be chosen of him to do special things for him. It will never matter what we look like, what we have or what we know, because when God chooses his people, he equips them to do the job he wants them to do. He can take a stammering spokesman and make him the greatest leader of the Jewish people. He can take a ruddy child shepherd and make him the greatest king of the Israelites. And he can do great things through us as well.

HOLD YOUR HEAD UP TO THE SKY

In July 2002 I attended a concert by the African Children's Choir of Uganda. This marvelous choir of children from ages seven to thirteen consists of those who have been orphaned through the ravages of war and disease. They have known only extreme poverty and hopelessness in their country, which has resulted in their having many psychological issues. Yet, as one of the attendants announced, being in the choir has raised their self-esteem immeasurably. Although participating in music has been known to do that, I think that something else contributed as well. At the end of the concert, the host pastor asked the children if they had a favorite Bible verse, and they all raised their hands enthusiastically, desiring to quote theirs. Then several began to speak about how much Jesus loved them. Many of their songs confirmed this belief in them, and that is the reason for their renewed hope for life and living. For the fact that God loves us is the single most consistent truth that will and can turn around the thought process of an individual, regardless of what she has seen or endured.

The psalmist says, "I will lift up mine eyes unto the hills, from whence cometh my help. My help cometh from the LORD" (Psalm 121:1-2). If we are to ever know our true value as women, it must come from God. We must look to him and only him as the Source of our self-esteem, value and identity. To look elsewhere is to cast our eyes into a dimmer version of who we are and what we can become. We must see ourselves reflected only in the eyes of God before we can truly see why he could and would choose us.

CHOSEN FOR PURPOSE

When God spoke to Jeremiah as a child, he told him that he had been chosen long before his birth. God told him three things had occurred even before his conception: (1) God knew him, (2) God sanctified him, and (3) God ordained him as a prophet. In choosing Jeremiah, God gave him three things: *identity, position* and *purpose*.

Nothing is more important than knowing who you are. It is this search for identity, for self, that sits at the core of much of the maladjusted behavior in our society. People don't know who they are. And a serious error is made when they allow those who have no real vested interest in them to mold their identity through shallow determinations based primarily on their own personal preferences and comfort zone. Who are you? It is this identity that will determine your place or your position in life. For you will seek to do those things that mirror the image that you have of yourself.

When Adam and Eve had eaten of the fruit in disobedience, they hid themselves. When God questioned them, they said that they were naked and ashamed. I love what God then asks them: "Who told you that you were naked?" (Genesis 3:10-11 NIV). Their self-image before that point had been reflected only in the eyes of God, and in his eyes there was no shame. They had always been naked, but their view of that nakedness as reflected in a sinless mindset was not one of shame. Their identity, how they saw themselves, was rapidly changing based on an improper influence. Who is it that determines your identity? They will surely also determine your position and your thoughts as to your purpose. We have to evaluate the source from which we draw our ideas and beliefs as to who we are and what we are capable of doing.

HERITAGE VERSUS HISTORY—DEEPER THAN JACOB'S WELL

The story of the woman of Samaria who met Jesus at Jacob's well is interesting to me, but for more than the reasons I have heard taught in the past (see John 4:6-29). Yes, this text teaches against segregation and discrimination in that one can point out how Jesus, a Jew, crossed typical lines of segregation by asking for and receiving a drink from a Samaritan woman. It teaches against religious and racial prejudices. I have heard teachings about the search for the indwelling of the Holy Spirit from this text. I have enjoyed dozens of sermons that have come from John's account of this story. But I recently saw something else that revealed to me a clearer understanding of our heritage versus our history.

Jacob's well was highly regarded and considered very deep. In fact, when cleaned out in 1935, it was found to be 138 feet deep.[4] It was this, as well as the fact that Jacob himself drank from that well, that was impressive to the woman and was a point of reference she used when talking with Jesus. It was this history that first kept her from seeing and hearing what Jesus was really saying to her when he offered her his water. She couldn't understand why Jesus would appear to be offering her something better than what Jacob had provided. "Are you greater than our father Jacob," she asked, "who gave us the well and drank from it himself, as did his sons and his flocks and herds?" (John 4:12 NIV). It was this history that limited her sight of what was really available to her. Could there be something and Someone greater than Jacob?

Women have surrendered themselves to the limitations of their history—the history of this country, that of their families and, for African American women, that of our race. We have even looked at faithful, holy women who have stood and gone before us and felt that to surpass them, or to even desire to have more or to do more than did they, would make us ungrateful for their sacrifice and labor or, even worse, would cause us to appear snobbish or superior.

There is a great history of leadership and worship in my family. There is a Levitical blessing over it that spans three generations: my father, four brothers and two nephews served as ministers and pastors to churches. They were all great leaders in the Lord's church, and it was expected of them. But it was also accepted that this blessing did not cover me. My love for the Word and desire to study it was not met by most people as being sincere, because I was defined by a different standard than the men in my family. I came from the same stock and had the same stuff in me but was not supposed to have the same desire to manifest it as the men did, simply because I was a woman.

After having preached for over fifty years, my father had a massive library of religious books, and he took great pride in it. He often said, "I am going to leave my books to my boys," meaning his preaching sons. However, they had been preaching themselves since they were teenagers and had amassed their own libraries and saw no value to what he would bequeath to them. I went to my father before his death and asked if I could be included in his will regarding his books. He merely laughed. When he died, my brothers did not want the books and my stepmother chose to lock them in an abandoned trailer in the country rather than let me have them because she felt that my father would not have approved. I loved and respected the depth of my historical well, but I knew that I had to go beyond *my Jacob* to seek what was deeper in me. I had to realize that much of my struggle when it came to leadership came from the influence of a male-dominated church environment and home influence.

When Jesus went into Nazareth, there were those who knew him and his people because it was his hometown. They knew Joseph the carpenter; Mary, his mother; his brothers James, Simon and others. They knew his sisters, who lived among them. So when Jesus returned there as the Son of God, they were offended by him, because he was stepping beyond *his Jacob* in their eyes (see Matthew 13:55-57). In limiting him by his family history, they limited themselves. He came offering works (healing and miracles) that they could not find in Jacob's well, and they would not drink of the water that he offered.

Jacob's water, though cool and deep, limits us by doctrines that would have us silently subject ourselves to abusive rhetoric that diminishes our true identity and heritage in Christ. Jacob's well would remind us of low expectations and gender preferences. Jacob's water would limit us by natural descent and bind us to circumstance and history. Jacob's water cannot quench the thirst in us to serve God fully and to use all of the gifts he has given us for him, his church, our communities and our country. Only Jesus' water can.

God gave Jeremiah identity and also positioned him to fulfill his purpose. It is important to be in the right place when God chooses you. In fact, God will position you himself and this positioning often takes us through a process. There may be things—difficult things—that you must endure in preparation for God to establish you in leadership. And when he chooses you for that, he will prepare you for the place where he will position you. Why? Because, like Jeremiah, God gave you purpose before you were born. Your destiny is that you live a fulfilled life, one that walks in authority and that impacts the lives of those around you. But once again we can greatly err when

KNOWN PURPOSE REVEALS THE PARTICULAR COMPONENTS GOD BUILT INTO YOU TO ENABLE YOU TO ACHIEVE ALL THAT HE PREPARED FOR YOU.

Myles Munroe, *In Pursuit of Purpose*

we allow others to determine our destiny and limit our impact. Sometimes these others are not all serpents that aim to destroy you, but can be well-meaning friends who feel they know what's best for you. They can be parents and family who feel you are limited to what the family history allows or to a particular vision that they have for your life.

The parents of Condoleezza Rice loved her dearly and always believed that she would be someone great. However, their idea of greatness was built around her becoming a concert pianist, and they began to train her at age three to achieve that goal. But the dream of excelling in classical music may have been a desire within her parents—her mother, in particular, a music teacher—but it was not the seed that would germinate within their daughter Condoleezza. Yes, Condoleezza studied music diligently on the beautiful baby grand piano they purchased as a gift for her. But when she enrolled in college at fifteen, she would realize that there was something else burning within her and calling her forth to high achievement. She switched her studies from music to political science, became fluent in Russian and today sits as the highest-ranking African American female in the history of the United States as national security adviser to the president. Condoleezza loved her parents and her music, but she was chosen to be what loved her.

You do not measure up to the standards that others have set for you, but you meet those set by God, and he has chosen you. With the world at his disposal, with the brightest minds and fairest skin standing before him in lines that stretched from heaven to the furthest ends of the earth, he stopped by your mother's womb and picked you. You, a black woman who has seen and known the worst that society has to offer, have been chosen to lead in the greatest country of the world, at the command of your Creator. And you must take your place . . . because you are chosen and because you can.

QUESTIONS FOR REFLECTION AND DISCUSSION

1. Do you confidently see yourself as being chosen of God? In what does your confidence lie?
2. What makes you an ideal candidate for being used by God?
3. Do you see women as being fit or capable to lead in all areas of your community, country and church? Why or why not?
4. What self-esteem issues that relate to being African American and female can you see and acknowledge as having kept you from standing as a leader?
5. Have you received your identity, position and purpose from God? If not, from where have you received them?
6. What is the well from which you draw your waters of identity, purpose and potential? Does it match what God has destined for you?

2 RESPONDING TO THE CALL

*You've laid the foundation; you've sown the seed
And now it's time for you to lead.*

There is nothing more fundamental to freedom than choice. It is through choice that freedom is ultimately expressed. It is to this cause that Elizabeth Cady Stanton and Susan B. Anthony founded the suffrage movement to secure the right for white women to vote. It was for freedom that Martin Luther King Jr., Ralph Abernathy and other civil rights leaders marched and endured the severity of retaliation from "Bull" Connor and others so that they could secure the right of choice for all of us. For they knew well that as long as it was someone else's choice where we ate, went to the bathroom and drank our water, we were not free. Bondage is expressed most profoundly in our thoughts and subsequently exhibited in our actions. It is through our choices that we demonstrate both freedom and fear.

We are both created and chosen to lead, but if we fail to choose it for ourselves we will forever be left to the whim and will of others around us who are often not more talented or capable but more confident in themselves and more comfortable with expressing their desire to lead. The mantles of leadership in our world today, whether spiritual or secular, do not always rest on the best and the brightest. Leaders are often not the most anointed and gifted, and rarely are the positions of leadership held by those who are reluctant to lead. Sometimes we are left to choose leaders who have already chosen to lead us.

Nowhere is this more evident than in politics and religion, especially in some urban areas. The desire to lead and the gall to take the necessary steps to do so often are the dominant qualifications in those who run our public offices—and even in those who grace our pulpits. More often than not, these are men who fall short of or barely fit the basic needs of leadership. Yet they are consistently chosen over women who may far excel them in every area. Sometimes this can be attributed to sexism and the lack of desire for fairness in leadership positions. But in many areas we must question what appears to be a lack of interest on behalf of women to take the reins of leadership and authority; women seem content to sit and not stand.

STANDING IS NOTHING NEW TO YOU

The fact that African American women have what it takes to lead is seen in our history as well as in our ability to survive the everyday drama of our lives. No one has to do more with less than we. No one has to overcome greater obstacles and withstand stronger struggles than we. But we do it successfully and consistently, time and time again. Necessity has forced us to invent things that we do not patent and create things for which we may never take the credit or claim copyright. But we are the ultimate survivors.

At seven years old, Erica Pratt demonstrated the survival instinct that is so common in black females that it appears almost inherent. Kidnapped by two abductors in Philadelphia and held captive in a stale basement of an abandoned house, she single-handedly freed herself by chewing through the tape binding her arms and legs, smashing through a window and then calling to nearby playing children for help. The police marveled not only at her ability to get away with just minor injuries but also at her remarkable poise and composure in the aftermath. "She's an amazing little girl," Chief Inspector Robert Davis said.[1] *She's a black woman in the making,* I thought.

Be It unto Me

As African American women, we can relate well to Mary, Jesus' mother. Poor, single and pregnant. Uneducated and without any real skills for taking care of herself. Her culture said she needed a man, for it was only through his existence that she had value. So what would God need with someone like this? Why would she be his choice when it is not likely that she would be anyone else's? Yet, not only did he choose her, she chose him. It had to be hard for her to believe. It had to be difficult for her to conceive that she would actually be the one forever hailed "blessed among all women" (Luke 1:42), yet she decided to pursue what she possessed. And in faith she made a choice to be chosen. Knowing that she would never again fit into the typical description of women, that she would be used as an example of the unique and strange phenomenon of the virgin birth, that some would laugh and others would forever doubt, she said yes.

Now It's Time to Stand out Front

There can be proclamations over us and prophecies given to us, but until we choose to become what God has created us to be, what he has called forth in us, we will never come to know the fullness of our potential and will withhold from the world our greatest gift. It will never matter who sings our praises or trumpets our cause; we must take the baton and in commanding fashion say yes to leading the choir.

> LEADERSHIP IS SELDOM OFFICIAL.
>
> **John C. Maxwell**

So often we have been the *unofficial* leaders. We have sat in pews and helped illiterate men read Scriptures from the pulpit. We have prepared sermons for men to preach. Some of us have been relegated to sitting in hidden places with microphones to assist in the praise and worship services, because we were not allowed as women to stand up front. How long have we been assistant pastors, assistant principals, assistant managers and deputy chiefs of staff, when we and everyone else knew that the bulk of the work and the major decisions often came from us? We have quietly acquiesced to these lesser positions, accepting our roles of responsibility but allowing others, usually our men, to receive the authority, respect and compensation that should have been our own.

Typically we did this to survive, to keep our homes stable and the egos of our men intact. So when we saw these men in authority, we gladly submitted ourselves to them, believing that it was better for all of us if they, and not us, led. This has happened more often in our churches than anywhere else. It has been in the black church where our men received their validation as leaders and held their power. And even though women have always outnumbered them two, three and sometimes four to one, we have never assumed the roles of leadership in our churches in numbers that have equaled our membership or mirrored our skills, gifts and abilities to do so. We have made a choice to let men have spiritual authority over us regardless of what God has called us to do.

YOU AIN'T NO CHICKEN!

Dennis P. Kimbro gives a wonderful illustration of an eagle egg that is found by a hen. The hen takes it home and with tender care brings it to life. Because the eagle is born into a chicken environment, it acts like a chicken, thinks like a chicken and has chicken ambitions. It does not look like a chicken, however, and becomes embarrassed and ashamed at its distinct features, which are much bigger and broader than the other chickens. But one day an eagle soars over where the young bird is playing with the other chicks. The shadow cast over them by the mighty wings of the eagle catches the attention of the younger eagle, who is impressed and awed by such strength in flight. He thinks how great it would be if he could be like that. Sensing the dilemma of the young bird, the large eagle swoops down to the ground and yells at him, "Boy, you ain't no chicken. You're an eagle!"[2] Created and designed to soar into the skies and to sit atop great mountains, the young bird was using its strong talons to merely scratch for worms in the ground. Until it acknowledged the choice to fulfill its eagle potential, it was content to be as a chicken.

IT REALLY IS UP TO US

There will always be those who will suggest to us that we are chickens when they fully know—and they fear we will believe—that we are eagles. Some of us have looked beyond the chicken environment that has molded us and we have felt a call to soar into the heavens. But we have waited for the release from others, hoping that they too would validate this desire by saying to us, "You ain't no chicken. You're an eagle!" But it really is up to us—and only us—to walk into our created being. We simply need to make the choice in thought, first, and then in action to reflect the eagle in us. It cannot matter if we are not assigned a leadership role, for leadership is assumed far more than it is assigned. I'm sure you know many examples of those who have received the mantle of another with blessing and even the laying on of hands, only to never walk in the authority of the position.

I clearly remember sitting at the homegoing services of a very popular and much-loved bishop in the Detroit area. His death was sudden and unexpected. At this service, his son moved all of us by saying that his father had just recently shared his vision with him so that he could carry on the work. Then much to the surprise of the audience, he said that he was going to deliver his father's eulogy because the work that he left required a leader, and he may as well start that day. He did not receive the assignment and was not confirmed as pastor of that church to succeed his father until many months later, but he assumed the authority of the leadership that very day. He has been respected and highly regarded in that role, and the church has gone on to grow and prosper as they brought to pass the vision that the bishop had shared with his son.

TAKE YOUR PLACE

It would be right for us to be assigned and offered positions and titles that would promote us into our rightful places as leaders, but that may not soon happen. We cannot wait until then to prepare ourselves for the positions. It must start today and it must begin with our beliefs that we are the leaders we were created to be. We must make an internal choice to lead.

See it! We must *perceive* our place as being at the top, in charge, in control and with authority. For if we cannot see it ourselves, we will have a difficult time casting an image that can be respected by others. My motto is, "If you can't see it before you see it, you'll never see it!" There is a Scripture that supports this: "What things soever ye desire, when ye pray, believe that ye receive them and ye shall have them" (Mark 11:24). You must believe that you have it before you even ask. See it before you see it.

As African American women we must first alter the paradigm in our minds as to what leadership is and who should be in those positions. We must see ourselves as black women sitting atop corporate boards, in judgeships, pulpits, hospitals and universities. We cannot be celebratory when we see just *one,* because the fact is that there ought to be *some.* Our vision of leadership must be inclusive of our sisters and not just an isolated place for us. Our choice to lead must begin with a new archetype of leadership and an expression of freedom through changed mindsets that will nurture and encourage the leader in all of us. When we look at the African American woman who has risen to great heights in her field, we cannot applaud it as if she is the only woman capable of such a feat. We must celebrate instead her vision of self, her drive and her willingness to make the necessary sacrifices for the accomplishment. And we must see it as an opportunity for others to follow behind—or even to sit alongside her.

I remember the first time I attended the worship services at Abyssinia Church, where Dr. Iona E. Locke served as pastor. I had witnessed only a couple of women as preachers and had never seen a woman stand in commanding fashion as the leader of a church. My first impression of the worship service left me spellbound, and I called a friend who was an assistant pastor at another church and told him that he had to come with me the next Sunday because I had stumbled on something he needed to see. The real truth is that I had not stumbled upon it, but had been led of God there because it was something that I desperately needed to see. I needed to see visibly a woman stand boldly in her calling, because it liberated me to seek my own. It strengthened my resolve in working to build Great Heritage Ministries, which I had founded years before, and it gave me the boldness to move out and onward in my work to encourage and empower women.

Secure it! We must *prepare* for our place at the top. Our being created and chosen for leadership cannot replace our need to be qualified for it. Some people have often spoken of those who have reached high goals and known great success as being lucky. They try to excuse others' accomplishments as being by chance, as being in part because of their place in life or their meeting a certain person. But those who are so successful and accomplished know that it was more than luck that got them where they are. In fact, many have defined luck as *preparation meeting opportunity*. When others have perceived them as being lucky, they know rather that they have prepared for the moment and thus grasped the opportunity afforded them.

I have been able to master fears in my life, with one exception. I am intimidated only by moments that find me unprepared. Preparation is the key to all success. Coach Bobby Knight has said, "The will to succeed is important. But more important is the will to prepare." Those we have looked upon as overnight success stories are never such. A further investigation shows long hours of energy focused on accomplishing great feats when others were not noticing their work. We will be successful leaders in equal fashion to our preparation to lead. *We must prepare against promise*: when there is no guaranteed position, we must still develop our potential to lead. *We must prepare against pressing*: there will be times in which we will be pressed into leadership because of need. Often we can foresee this need and should prepare ourselves for it. *We must prepare against prejudice*: it cannot matter to us that there are those who think we cannot or should not lead because of our race or gender. We must prepare ourselves based on our knowledge of who we are and the unlimited possibilities that face us.

> THE PROOF OF THE DESIRE IS IN THE PURSUIT.
>
> **Mike Murdock,** *Dream Seeds*

Shadow it! in light of our preparation, we must *pursue* our place in leadership. It is incumbent on us to pursue what we believe that God desires we possess. Ambitious women are looked on as almost being indecent. Some people used defamatory terms to talk of Hillary

Clinton desiring to become President of the United States. It was as if she were committing some major transgression by her desire alone. She was made to defend herself constantly and to deny that she was using a seat in the Senate to prepare for a presidency—something that is accepted and almost expected of the men who would choose to run. Assertiveness and aggressiveness is slapped down in women by the same hands that applaud it in men. But we cannot allow this to abort our ambition, simply because some are not comfortable with our confidence in becoming what we are created to be. Because we are often standing in the background of others, we must use this opportunity to shadow, or study and model, them as we define our own leadership. Despite the insult and recrimination that may be hurled at us, we have every right to pursue our place at the top.

I literally shouted for joy when I heard that former senator Carol Mosely Braun was going to run for President of the United States in 2004. I was ecstatic for several reasons, one of which is that she was an African American female seeking the highest office in the land. She had held various political positions that allowed her to prepare for such a run, but my excitement was in the fact that she had the fortitude and confidence to choose to do something and to pursue it, despite the fact that few would believe that she should or that she would ever successfully accomplish it.

Seize it! We must never be too reticent or fearful to *possess* our place as leaders. At the proper time, we must occupy the place for which we have planned, prayed and prepared. Perceiving our place, preparing for it and pursuing it will be for naught if we fail to take possession of it. The thrill cannot just be in the pursuit. We are not seeking moral victories where we can be proud of noble efforts that fall short. We want to possess the promise of the seed implanted in us.

The Israelites had sojourned in the wilderness outside the land that was promised to them. When God felt it was time for them to take possession, he told Moses to send twelve men to see what they would ultimately possess. However, in spite of their having prepared themselves for the land and having pursued it through their journey, they could not possess their promise because of fear. They saw less in themselves than they saw in their promise, and they lost their possession. Caleb urged them to have courage and faith by reminding them that they were *well able* to be victorious and to claim what was rightfully theirs. But they did not choose to possess the very thing that God had prepared and promised to them (see Numbers 13:25-33).

I love the twelve-step method that is so successful in breaking addictions in lives. When I was a chaplain intern at Veterans Hospital in Detroit, I was privileged to teach one of the steps in the chemical dependence center. This program has successfully transformed many an alcoholic, gambler and drug addict over the years. However, its success is predicated upon the choices made by the person who is addicted, and the very first choice must be to recognize the addiction and to take control of their lives. They are taught that there is a better way to live and a better path to take, but until they make the choice to have that life and to walk that path, it will never be something they possess.

There is a path that calls for us to leave emblazed footprints that can be followed by others into great service for the world. There is a promise for us to pursue that will bring a better life not only for ourselves but also for our communities, our cities and our country. Charles de Gaulle said, "Men are only great if they are determined to be so." As African American women we must step up to the plate and declare with confidence and conviction what we have seen, prepared for and pursued as belonging to us—and possess it. Our first step to leadership begins with our choice. We will lead if we determine to do so, for it really is up to us.

QUESTIONS FOR REFLECTION AND DISCUSSION

1. In what ways can you relate to Mary? What does it take for you to say, "Be it unto me . . . "?

2. At what times have you waited for validation from others before you decided to seek or assume a position of leadership?

3. Consider the ways in which you have assumed positions of "unofficial leadership."

4. What have you been able to see yourself doing? Have you begun preparing yourself for what you see? Have you taken steps to pursue and possess what you have seen?

3 FACING CRISIS

Stand with dignity, strength and grace.

*L*eaders are prepared on the stage of adversity. It is in the valley of criticism, derision and disparagement that one sees a true reflection of who she is and on what she stands. This is a place that is all too familiar to African American women. So often we have made our beds and our homes between rocks and hard places, sometimes by choice but mostly by force. Usually in this valley there are no hands that applaud your decisions. There are no choruses to sing your approval. It is hollow, with only the resounding echoes of your convictions to keep you company. It is here you learn to be numb to numbers, for you may have to walk alone. You must become deaf to distractions so that you can remain clearly focused on what lies ahead. You must ignore the polls of public opinion and the cry of the crowd, for neither of those are true measuring units to what you can withstand and what you can overcome. They may test and try you but it will be that intangible spirit within you that will determine your ability to stand.

As African American women who lead, we are often forced to carry our usual burden of trying to be all things to everybody in our lives, juggling enormous responsibility and dealing with our emotional needs, often alone. This creates for us situations of fatigue and stress. I have heard some men describe us as angry, bitter women. But whereas there are those among our ranks, I would say that what they really see in us is good, old-fashioned fatigue. The struggle of our

lives and the manner in which we have to go about securing and accomplishing those things that we desire have taken a toll on us. We
are tired women. We would love to have an easier life. Most African
American women would welcome
help. But all too often we are doing
things without the full circle of support that would make our choices
and chores less than cumbersome.
There are times in which we would
love to run from the demands upon
us, if but for a moment. Yet what we

> YOU CANNOT ESCAPE THE
> RESPONSIBILITY OF
> TOMORROW BY EVADING
> IT TODAY.
> **Abraham Lincoln**

find is that in our most difficult and trying times, leadership does not
take a vacation. The expectation on us is that we will find and tap
into an everlasting reservoir of strength and somehow find a way to
carry on and carry others with us as well. And in amazing fashion and
with uncanny consistency, we more than often rise to that level.

THE POWER TO OVERCOME

We are a people who have overcome so much. "We shall overcome"
has been our battle cry since the early days of the civil rights movement. We preach it, we talk it, and we sing it. We have overcome so
many obstacles and dealt with so much that it has been looked upon
as our innate ability. Struggle is intrinsic to our history, and for many
of us, strain is a part of our daily grind. Unfortunately, when difficulty
is so common to one's existence, some acquiesce to it and become re-
sistant to the demands for continual fight. It is at these times when we
surrender ourselves to those things that will make us more comfortable with the struggle: drugs, alcohol, gambling and illicit sexual relationships. We turn to things that will simply make us forget or feel
better during the battle, instead of calling on our fortitude to fight.

As African American women we must first overcome improper perception. Paradigms have been established in this country as to what is beautiful, what is strong and what is smart, among other things. We have used these models to determine the worthiness of individuals to have and to do certain things, and it has been an improper measurement for the true value of people. Outside of sports and entertainment, the American paradigm has not included us. Therefore expectations have been established for us and the bar for our achievement has been lowered. All too often we have accepted this, and it has limited and in many ways damaged our perception of ourselves.

It seems that most of us never really come to know or understand just who we are in God and the power that we have as a result. There are many examples of this in Scripture, none more common than the Israelites, who would not walk into their promise because ten men saw them as being too inferior to do so. Having been in the wilderness eating manna and quail, they had the opportunity to go into a land that flowed with milk and honey and that offered them all the pleasures of life. But when Moses sent twelve spies into that land, ten of them returned saying there were giants in that land, and "we were in our own sight as grasshoppers, and so we were in their sight." Interesting enough, they stated that they were as grasshoppers in "their own sight," and so they also were in their enemies'. They had projected their improper perception on and to others, which is what we always do (see Numbers 13:26-33).

We African American women have heard ourselves referred to in the most degrading and insulting terms. We are the objects of scorn by rap artists, who consider us to be little more than sex toys to be used and abused at will. We see images of ourselves that do not always reflect us in positive terms or, at best, simply limit us to certain duties or roles in life. Because we have not always challenged them, we have received them as truth. And for many African American women and society in general, perception has become reality.

But there must be a spirit in us, akin to that which was in Caleb, that lets us see what the others see on the outside, yet still know that there is something greater on the inside, and so declare with certainty, "We are well able to overcome." We must overcome what we hear from others and defer instead to what God has said about us. We must battle what we have even come to believe about ourselves. For if we do not overcome the enemy within our own thinking, we will never have the strength to withstand our most difficult times.

CRISIS CRYSTALLIZES YOUR CALL

Shortly after my divorce I got an e-mail message from a former student expressing his concern, and it was very tender to me. In responding, I assured him that I was going to be okay. But I said that if it was true that "adversity is the thing that introduces a man to himself," then I had indeed met Sylvia and found her to be a woman worth knowing. The difficulties of a divorce after nineteen years of marriage were beyond what I had imagined or expected. I could not even describe my feelings and could not understand my emotions. In the beginning, all I knew was to keep on going and to continue to do what I had always done. But what I had always done was to take care of other people's needs and to help them through difficult times. Consequently those people in my life responded to me during my time of need as if nothing had changed and continued to make the same demands on me. They didn't see or understand that I lacked the strength or the mental and emotional fortitude to handle the dramatic changes and stress of my own life, much less theirs.

So many times I wanted to escape the pressure that came with the adjustment of my new life. I had gone from a comfortable lifestyle to struggling in a manner that was foreign to me. The loss of my home, income, health insurance and good credit rating was devastating. It left me reeling, feeling vulnerable and insecure. I battled with depression and found but a few sympathizers, in part because I had been a very private person and had never complained about any marital problems. A number of Christian women surprised me by letting me know that, regardless of what went on, I needed to make whatever adjustments were necessary, keep my mouth shut and stay put. Their advice was not based on their interpretation of Scripture regarding divorce but was merely their input on "how to keep your stuff." I found talking to others merely exacerbated my grief and brought no relief. So, as I have done often in my life, I suffered in silence and continued on. But in spite of my desire to withdraw from people to seek solace only for myself, I was never completely able to do so because I had learned that crises, conflict and controversy serve to crystallize your calling and not to cut it off.

Through this crisis, I saw more clearly that God has placed in me a call to help the desperate and downtrodden people of the world. Advocacy runs through my veins, and it is very difficult for me to turn away from those who are in true need. I never have to look for them because they seem to find me. God sends people to me who are alone and rejected, unable to find help anywhere else. I have been called to psychiatric wards for those needing someone to come pray with them and to see them through when they have not desired to let others know where they were. I have had to step in to help only children bury both of their parents or to help mothers deal with the multiple deaths of their children. When I felt I could deal only with myself, calls from women with more desperate needs than my own continued to come. I knew I could not turn a deaf ear to their call. I was forced to put aside the fact that I was struggling to barely eat and to deal with those who didn't think they could even live. Through consistent prayer and meditation on the Word of God, I was reminded of those Scriptures from which I could draw strength for myself and for those to whom I ministered. My calling was confirmed through my personal crisis, and it caused me to remain faithful to what I know that God desires me to be and do. Adversity and strife really do introduce you to yourself. You find out who you are. And you come to know what you are made for.

It was during my most difficult times that God led me to begin a special ministry to uplift and empower women. The very thing that I needed in my life I was moved to do for others. I founded Breakfast And A Word, a series of monthly breakfasts where women of all backgrounds, cultures and denominations would come together for times of refreshing, inspiration and empowerment. When the idea was first breathed into my spirit, I thought it was a wonderful thing for another woman to do. But the woman that I had in mind was not moving in that direction, and I was frustrated about it. In prayer God revealed that it was my vision, my call and not hers, and I needed to move quickly to do what he was charging me to do. My obedience to the call on my life, even in the midst of conflict and crisis, served to strengthen me, that I might endure that period of hardship.

RESPOND AND DON'T REACT

There are certain steps that I take in dealing with conflict, crisis and controversy. The first is that I always try to respond to them and not to react to them immediately. Most people know that it is usually difficult to get an emotional rise out of me, because I have trained myself to respond to things and people and not to react to them. For me, that means I will respond according to what I want to take place and not necessarily what I know has just occurred. Response is proactive.

To react to things said or done is often to match its intensity in emotions and actions, which may or may not be productive for you in the end. Response tends to allow you to control yourself and therefore the situation. Admittedly I have some sensitive and tender spots that, if pricked, may bring a more ready response than others. But I have come to learn that you have an advantage over the problem situation when you are able to respond to it instead of reacting to it.

RECOGNIZE THE ENEMY

When the apostle Paul wrote to the church in Ephesus, he warned them about the warfare they would have to endure, and he wanted them to be prepared. He pointed out who the enemy is: "For our struggle is not against flesh and blood, but against the rulers, against the authorities, against the powers of this dark world and against the spiritual forces of evil in the heavenly realms" (Ephesians 6:12 NIV). This is often taken lightly or overlooked. But it is extremely important to know who and what you are up against. So often we waste our energies fighting the wrong things. Most of the time we are fighting people, when rarely is it people who are the enemies.

When I was younger and integrating the public schools in Georgia, I had to battle the evils of racism. As I became older, there were situations when I still had to fight racism, but sexism was added to it. Through painful experiences I was able to see that this really was the same demonic spirit, which is fed by ignorance and prejudice. That single realization helped me to deal patiently and in love with the people involved, while I fought and detested the spirit that possessed them. Paul said plainly that our fight is not against flesh and blood (not against humans) but against the rulers, authorities and powers of darkness. We think it is against people because of the effect these things have on people. However, when we resign ourselves to fighting people and not the powers that rest on them, two things happen: we lose the war and we end up bitter. Our enemies will be those things (spirits) that will cause us to doubt, which will weaken our resolve and make us lose sight of our priorities. It is against *them* that we must fight and stand.

REMEMBER YOUR PAST ACHIEVEMENTS

When I am faced with very difficult situations, I consider them thoroughly first to see if any part of the problem is recognizable to me. I really do believe that there is nothing new under the sun and I don't believe in fighting the same war twice, especially if I have been victorious in it before. Therefore I dissect the situation to see if I can call on a pattern or method I successfully used to resolve something similar in the past. If it is a totally new problem, I remember my successes in the past as a way to remind myself of my ability to handle conflict. When I do that, it strengthens my faith in God, with and by whom I have been able to face and handle all things, and it increases the self-confidence that I need to take care of the problem.

After leaving my teaching position in Texas and coming to Michigan to marry, I taught for several years at a Christian school in the metropolitan Detroit area. After several years of teaching, I left to pursue song writing full time but remained connected to the school by serving on its board of directors. We had three different locations, and one of them had an emergency need for a principal shortly after the school year began. The board looked to me to provide leadership through that difficult time, and I agreed to do so.

I assumed the position of principal and remained throughout the school year. But I walked into a situation that was hostile, to say the least. Whereas our other two locations were more integrated, only about 5 percent of the student body of this school was of African American descent. There were no African American teachers and only two black females there: a lunchroom aide and a preschool aide. My presence there as the leader was a shock to the school's entire system and their way of doing things, and I was not well received. Drama ensued from my first day at that campus and continued for weeks. With persistent tests by parents, teachers and students, I saw that I was succumbing to the stress, and my confidence in my leadership skills began to wane. I knew that I had to do something to rebuild my faith in who I was and what I was able to do.

I had been an accomplished person all of my life and had received many awards and commendations. However, I had just packed them all away in boxes and never had displayed them, even in my home. One evening after everyone had left the school, I lined the four walls of my office with plaques from top to bottom. I laughed while I was doing it, because it truly was a gaudy sight. But it worked! I thought it would simply remind me of my success and strengthen my confidence and resolve for the work that I had to do as principal. And it did that. Every time I walked into that office I was reminded that I was a woman of achievement, regardless of what was said of me. But something else occurred as well. Every student, teacher and parent changed in their approach to me. They also responded to the positive environment that I had created for myself, and many of the power struggles began to decrease.

There will always be times when those who think you are not the one to be in the position of authority and leadership will challenge you. It is then that you must remind yourself of who you are and what you have done in the past to prepare you for the conflict and challenge that you presently endure.

REHEARSE YOUR TESTIMONY

I have always been struck by the fact that God consistently told the Israelites to remember their days in Egypt and how he had brought them out of bondage (see Exodus 13:14). He wanted memorials established, and he told them to talk about it and to tell their children and grandchildren. It wasn't the problem (Egypt) that he wanted them to be reminded of; it was the deliverance. He wanted them never to forget the covenant that they had and to be ever reminded of their relationship with him.

As African Americans we seem to have a problem with slavery. We are almost as uncomfortable with discussing it as is white America. Movies made about that ugly time in our country's history are not usually as well attended as others. And ratings for TV programs that document our struggles lag behind those of less serious dramas or comedies. Some of us become angry and bitter when watching the brutality that we endured, but I seek out the opportunities to revisit this period of my history because I am encouraged and strengthened by it. I have membership in the Museum of African American History in Detroit, and I often go there just to look at the replica of the slave ship and to gaze into the dark, desperate eyes of the slaves that peer out of the bottom of that ship. I am neither angry nor bitter with these daunting scenes, because more than the bondage, I see the deliverance. Even though for many of us the bondage remains in our minds, our successes as a people and especially as women—what we have been able to accomplish through and by the hand of God—can be celebrated.

I refuse to curse my wilderness experiences. Instead I try to embrace the lessons that I learn in the valley, because they can serve as steppingstones in my journey to the mountaintop. We will overcome conflict and crisis and continue to lead when we remember that we have a testimony and when we rehearse what God has done through us. It is our testimony of our journey through the depths of despair that will carry us to the heights of exhilaration, personal triumph and achievement. John wrote in Revelation and reminds us that in our war with Satan, we overcome by the blood of Christ and the word of our testimony (see Revelation 12:11). In our times of challenge and crisis, we must remember and rehearse our testimony.

REINFORCE AND REESTABLISH YOUR PRIORITIES

The main detrimental thing that conflict and controversy are able to accomplish is to cause us to lose our focus. We then begin to concentrate on those things that are of lesser importance, and we waste precious time and energy in the process. When we lose our focus, we fight unnecessary battles and we give in to our egos, often doing things that do little to nothing to advance the real goals we need to accomplish.

During my time as principal, I often walked through the cafeteria area to talk with the children. One day a first grader jumped from her table and ran toward me. I cringed because her mouth and fingers were full of peanut butter and jelly, and I knew she was about to share her lunch with my clothing. Sure enough, she grabbed me around my legs, looked up at me and said, "I love you so much, Mrs. Cobb, I could take you to show and tell." Suddenly the peanut butter stains didn't matter and in a split second the reason I was there was brought to the forefront of my thinking. I could choose to focus my time and energies on power struggles with the adults, but I was really there for the children.

When we realize that much of what we do is for and about those generations after us, our perspective about our own situations change. We then realize that many of the struggles between adults are centered on ego and personality and not on the issue at hand.

Focusing on the children will make us more radical in our fight for equality, for we would want them to know all the liberties to which they are entitled. It will move us not only to confront controversy in our lives, but also to embrace it. I have never believed that leaders should attempt to avoid all controversy. There ought to be some things that we stand for and do that will be challenged and discussed and that will bring about positive change as a result. Instead of trying to avoid a baptism of fire, sometimes we need to stoke the embers.

Bayard Rustin was an expert strategist and activist in the struggle for human rights and economic justice. He was instrumental in every major civil and human rights movement in the United States for over fifty years and served in pivotal roles in forcing the attention to injustice in America. He was passionately committed to freedom and justice. It was his background in the theory and tactics of nonviolent resistance that proved to be invaluable to Martin Luther King Jr. It was Rustin who worked with A. Phillip Randolph in organizing the great March on Washington that served as the platform for King's memorable and historic "I Have a Dream" speech. Rustin believed in what he called "angelic troublemaking" and often did things that he knew were against the accepted norms for African Americans, so as to incite a response from the powers that be to bring attention to the injustices that he hated so much. Long before Rosa Parks was arrested and the Montgomery Bus Boycott began, Rustin sat in the "whites only" section of a bus while traveling in Tennessee and was brutally beaten and arrested. When the police were demanding that he move from his seat, Rustin looked at a young white child and said, "If I move, then this child will never know that injustice is taking place here."[1] To Rustin, the fight for equality was not for himself and his contemporaries alone. It was about the children, the generations that would come after him. This served as the focus of his fight.

When I was much younger, controversy bothered me—until I understood its impact on me and others. For me to try to avoid it meant that I would have to *not* do things that I believed in and that were for the betterment of myself and others. For me to withstand controversy often brought enlightenment and understanding to others. When this was clearly revealed to me, I no longer avoided controversy but began in many ways to embrace it.

In the church where I previously worshiped, women were not typically permitted to speak in churches when men were present. In fact, when I would take my high school choir into churches for programs, there were times when I was told that I had to select one of my young male students to announce the songs that we would sing. On one occasion I was told that I had to keep my back to the audience and never turn around. Emotionally this was not good for me. Regardless of the Scripture references used to teach me "my proper place," it did not settle well in my psyche or my spirit. When I left that school and formed my own ensemble, I not only would announce the songs that we would sing, but many times would take the opportunity to tell about the inspiration that led me to write it. I knew well and could tell by looking in the faces of many of the men that this was not acceptable to them. But it was what I saw in the faces of the women that made me know that I had to continue to speak. Afterward they would embrace me and whisper in my ear for me to "keep speaking" and "keep standing." Many would simply say thank you. But it was the younger girls who would sometimes write me notes and letters that made me know that there were things that I would need to do that would bring discomfort to me but deliverance for others. I knew that I could never run from controversy and still lead.

REFLECT ON TRUTH

I have two signs on opposite walls of my office that read, "Things are *not* as they appear!!!" It is important to me to read that every day because, with so much happening in and around me, I realize that I could get swept away by the trauma and drama of it all. The signs serve to remind me that even if things look one way, there is likely another side to it that will bring balance and restore hope. When things appear to be unmanageable and out of control, there is always a way to get things done. When it seems that so many are against me and I am surrounded by forces that would take me out, I pause to consider that I am also circled by angels and a cloud of witnesses that are pulling for me to succeed.

It reminds me of the story of Elisha the prophet, who is surrounded by horses and chariots and a strong force that would do him harm. His servant becomes alarmed and excited at seeing this multitude against them. But Elisha tells him, "Those who are with us are more than those who are with them" (2 Kings 6:16 NIV). The servant could not understand what was being told to him because of what appeared real according to what he was seeing. But there was something else that had to be revealed to him. Elisha asked God to open the servant's eyes so that he could see the unseen reality of their situation. When God did so, he saw "hills full of horses and chariots of fire all around Elisha" (v. 17).

Sometimes we lose sight of truth when we are embroiled in conflict and controversy. Or our definition of truth can be altered to reflect the opinions of those who have control over us and our situations. But regardless of what we are facing and what we see or hear, there is an unseen reality for godly women that reminds us, "Greater is he that is in [us], than he that is in the world" (1 John 4:4).

Reflecting on truth will keep you from becoming bitter about those painful experiences in your past, and it will serve to put them into proper perspective with the unseen reality that is working in your life. But it is our human nature to remember the negative more than the positive. For every ten people who will compliment us, we will often walk away with the stinging criticism of the one negative comment ringing in our ears. It is more likely that the ten compliments reflect the real truth, but our proclivity is to hear the one criticism clearer than the compliments.

Although I have been challenged greatly by men regarding leadership, I've had to reflect on the true relationships that I have enjoyed with men so as to maintain the proper attitude about them. I have never heard a complaint from a man under my leadership regarding my leadership style or the manner in which I have interacted with him. Long after our working relationships have ended, they have—more than the females—sought me out for counsel and friendship. In the same manner I have had to reflect on the true relationships that I have had with white Americans. I have had to remember that the times in which my life was embroiled in racism and discrimination do not properly reflect the complete picture of my interactions with all Caucasians.

Reflecting on truth will help you to forgive those who have attempted to harm you, because it will remind you that they failed in what they were trying to do. It will keep you in remembrance of God's Word that promises, "No weapon that is formed against thee shall prosper" (Isaiah 54:17). Reflecting on truth will also remind you of your own shortcomings and need for God's mercy. You will be less likely to withhold forgiveness from others when you are mindful of your own need to be forgiven.

I taught a class on forgiveness and in my research I learned that the Greek meaning of the word *forgive* is to "unloose, untie and to free."[2] We keep people in bondage when we will not forgive them.

But we also keep ourselves enslaved to bitterness and hatred. Two years after my divorce I wrote my ex-husband a letter and told him that I had put the ugliness of our divorce behind me and had made a decision to hold on to only the good memories that I had of us at our best. When I wrote the letter, I was still going through very difficult times that had resulted from the divorce. But I knew that unless I was free of the hurt and pain, I would not move on, because becoming bitter would prohibit my becoming better. I had to forgive and loose him so that I could free me.

Controversy, conflict and crisis can tie us up and prohibit us from being the leaders we should be, if we become so distracted by them that we lose sight of our priorities, fail to recognize the unseen realities and do not reflect on what is really true. As African American women we are always at a crossroad of choice regarding the direction we will take in response to tests and trials, which seem to be prevalent in our lives. More often than not, we choose to face them and overcome them and are rarely defeated by them. They serve instead to strengthen our resolve as women and as leaders, and they crystallize the call on our lives. They can also call into our remembrance women of our history like Harriet Tubman, Mary McLeod Bethune and Sojourner Truth, who consistently overcame controversy, crisis and conflict to establish themselves as leaders in response to the needs of their people and the cry of injustice. These same needs exist and, African American women, we must overcome crises, face our conflicts and confront controversies so that we may lead and respond to the cry of injustice in our land.

QUESTIONS FOR REFLECTION AND DISCUSSION

1. Reflect on the paradigms that you have held in the past for what is beautiful, smart and worthy of regard. Did you and others who

look like you fit that paradigm? How did this perception impact choices you've made for your life?

2. How has crisis, conflict or controversy crystallized your call? Have you been tested to the point where your character has been defined and your call made distinct?

3. In what ways have crises in your life helped you to serve others?

4. Compare the author's steps for dealing with crisis (respond and don't react, recognize your enemy, remember your past achievements, etcetera) with those that you have used. Is there one particular step that you feel could help you effectively deal with a difficult situation now?

4 ACTING WITH COURAGE

Stand on your history of sacrifice,
Of your courage to face adversity and strife.

$\mathcal{E}$very day we are presented with choices and opportunities to be courageous, and many times we bow our heads and sidestep the option because of our fears. The daily challenges we face are not those that would draw us into heroic demonstrations of physical prowess. They are not tests of mental and emotional endurance beyond what would be considered common. For in any situation that threatens the health and stability of our children, our families or ourselves, we somehow find the reservoirs of strength and courage and drink of them, enabling us to do things in ways that would normally be considered extraordinary. The opportunities that send us running, however, are those that call for us to be different, to stand away from the crowd and to isolate ourselves from the ordinary. Unfortunately it is here where we sit when we should stand, where we cower when we should confront.

Leadership is seen first in one's ability to overcome fear. Courage is a major component of being a leader. Nothing is more discouraging, disappointing and disheartening than to find yourself sitting at the feet of a cowardly leader. You can be certain that any group or organization that is headed by a fearful leader is one that is stagnant and struggling to keep up with the times. This body of people will never stand at the forefront of new ideas and will always be imitators of what others do. They will never know a cutting-edge experience because their leader will not take the risk to try something different. It will be difficult, if not impossible, to change things within your organization, for change represents the very thing that these people fear the most—the unknown.

The Courage to Be Called and Chosen

Many times the fear that one sees in the eyes of others is actually a fear of succeeding at what they have been called and chosen to do. There is as much a fear of success in people as there is a fear of failure, for the first thing success accomplishes is to set us apart. Often it isolates us from our friends and family, leaving us with few who would understand where we are and what we are doing. Success draws us to a higher level of responsibility and visibility, and it often makes us vulnerable to attacks from others. For this reason some people try to lead from the back of the pack, hiding behind a false humility that would place others up front while they called the shots from afar.

Jonah did not want to be chosen of God to speak to his people, so he ran instead of being obedient to the call on his life. But Jonah proved what many of us have learned: you can only run so far for so long. If we are to ever come to peace with ourselves we will have to reach a point of atonement with our spirit and our Creator, and with courage accept our call and destiny in life.

A Choice of Spirits

Courage and fear really are about spirits. When Joshua and Caleb went with the other ten spies to see the land God had promised the Israelites, those two stood alone against the others, who were overcome by the spirit of fear and who felt that they could not secure the land—and therefore the promise—God had for them. But the Bible says that Caleb "had another spirit with him" (Numbers 14:24), which enabled him to stand fearlessly and proclaim their ability to be victorious.

Fear is a noxious spirit. From this spirit of fear grows racism, sexism, poor self-esteem, ignorance and prejudice. Many times we respond to fear more than we do to facts, and so through our fears we make decisions that are ill-conceived and irrational. This spirit, which did not come from God (see 2 Timothy 1:7) goes against our creation as leaders and women of dominion and authority. Because God has given to us his Spirit—and fear and the Spirit cannot coexist—we typically do the unthinkable in dismissing the Spirit of God from among us when we receive the spirit of fear. Therefore we must make every effort to overcome, eradicate and break the spirit of fear in our lives so that we might have access to the power of God. There are four ways we can overcome fear so that we might live our destiny and have the courage to lead.

Fix your foundation. Fear is such a strong and often paralyzing emotion. It impedes progress and success, and keeps us stagnant, unable to free ourselves from yesterday's mistakes and failures to move on into the future. Often this fear arises when we place our beliefs and/or priorities in temporal things—that which is here today and gone tomorrow. As African American women who lead, we can ill afford to have our faith based on or rooted in those things created and controlled by people—those things that have no substance or sound foundation. Jesus taught the multitude on the mountain about the importance of proper foundations, using the examples of rock and sand. The wise will build on rock, so that she will be well grounded when the elements assail. The foolish, building on sand, will know failure and calamity, for her house will succumb to the weakness of her foundation (see Matthew 7:24-27). If our priorities are established upon and centered around materialism, jobs and temporal images, we have every reason to fear. They constitute a flimsy, shallow foundation.

However, a foundation built on the Word of God is a foundation of strength, power and confidence. It surpasses all other foundations; there are none else that can be laid to match or compare to it (see 1 Corinthians 3:11). This foundation yields faith that conquers fear.

Feed your faith. Especially as leaders, it is imperative that we remind ourselves daily, through prayer and Bible study, of the principles of our faith. We must ever call to our remembrance the covenant relationship that we share with God, as well as his faithfulness to it. Feeding our faith will starve the spirit of fear, just as starving our faith feeds the spirit of fear. Only one will be fed, will be nourished and grow. Fear and faith will not sustain each other. What we must understand is that the spirit of fear will feed on any negative energy and thoughts you may come in contact with. That spirit attracts them, and there are many things (TV, music, advertising, news, books, magazines and so on) that are designed to keep the spirit of fear fed to the point of glut. You don't have to make a decision to have that spirit fed. It will eat sumptuously without much assistance on your part. However, you must be proactive in feeding your faith. There needs to be a conscious effort to read, to consume, to study those things that will increase your faith and secure your relationship with God. A knowledge of self as established through the Word of God will build your confidence and give you the courage you need to lead.

Fellowship with the faithful. I have always appreciated God's command to the Israelites not to marry into the nations that were idolatrous because it would weaken their relationship with him. In a like manner, I have always believed that associations with those who don't believe in your vision of life and who do not share your moral commitments weaken the bond and link to the power that lies within you and beyond you. It must be stated that as Christians our primary goal is to share a positive testimony that will influence others toward a relationship with God. Therefore we should not disconnect ourselves from society in such a way that we will make no contribution to its betterment and will fail to serve as the influence that we should. At the same time, we need to find like-minded people with whom we can associate so that our faith in our calling and who we are as chosen vessels of God can flourish.

It is so interesting and helpful to consider Mary, the mother of Jesus, and her acceptance of being chosen of God to birth the King. As we have discussed, she was not unaware of the problems that she would face, or the ridicule and scorn. But she had the courage to be chosen and to say to God, "Be it unto me according to thy will" (Luke 1:38). Mary does something very interesting when she immediately goes to visit her cousin Elizabeth, for in Elizabeth she finds someone else who has been chosen of God for the extraordinary and in whom she would find understanding. When Mary enters into Elizabeth's home, the promise in Elizabeth begins to celebrate because it recognizes the promise in Mary (see Luke 1:41).

When you are chosen of God you cannot expect others who do not receive or understand their own calling to encourage you to walk into your destiny. In the solitude of your own thinking, you will have to decide that you will have the courage to be and do that for which you were created. And having made the decision to say yes to your potential, you will find that only those who have acknowledged and acquiesced to their own destinies will have the ability to celebrate you in yours.

To overcome and break the spirit of fear, you must reduce, diminish and rid yourself of the negative, nonbelieving influences that exist in your life and replace them with those positive, God-believing, faith-building supporters. Associate with and surround yourself with those who live boldly and courageously and whose spirits can celebrate the call on your life to lead.

Focus on the Savior. The story of Peter and his walk with Christ on the stormy seas is well known. When Peter saw Jesus approaching the disciples' ship, his faith moved him to join Jesus on the sea. As long as his mind and eyes were set on getting to Jesus, his feet were steady. However, when Peter became more focused on his surroundings than on the Savior, his fear superseded his faith and he began to drown (see Matthew 14:25-30). Fear is an ominous spirit that overshadows us and prohibits our growth and development because it hides us from the Source that would keep us fueled toward accomplishment. That Source is accessed through faith, and fear is a blockage to faith. For Christian African American women, our Source is Christ and it is through and by him that we are supplied with the strength, faith and courage to lead. If we allow fear to distract us so that we lose sight of him and his desire for our life, we will see instead those things that will weaken our tenacity and cause us to falter in our efforts to be the leaders that we are destined to be. The writer of Hebrews encourages us to "run with endurance the race" that is before us by "keeping our eyes on Jesus, on whom our faith depends from start to finish" (12:1-2 NLT).

THE COURAGE TO FACE CHALLENGES

One of the most courageous women in the history of our country was Harriet Tubman, a runaway slave who herself became a conductor of the Underground Railroad. She was called Moses and likened to him because over a ten-year period and through nineteen expeditions, she led some three hundred runaway slaves from the southern plantations to freedom in the north through the Underground Railroad.[1] Each trip challenged her physically and emotionally, and she was always under the threat of death. But Tubman knew that the possibility of dying was no challenge to the reality of living in bondage. She was unwavering in her belief that through death or determined effort she was going to be free. It was her dream and her goal of freedom for every slave that kept her fearlessly returning to the plantations year after year to help those still in bondage to know freedom. A quote in *The Liberator* was attributed to her: "I will not excuse nor will I retreat a single inch until the last slave breathes free."[2]

Facing challenges, small and monumental, is not new to the African American experience, and especially to its women. There really is no doubt as to our ability to deal with challenge; it is merely a question of our choice to do so. We will choose to face challenges and become leaders when we determine that the goal we want to meet and the vision we have for our lives and those we love outweigh those challenges. We have demonstrated over the years that we have the courage to face challenges, but it is not always our choice.

While David was yet a young lad and before he assumed his position as king, he had a chance meeting with a bully named Goliath. Merely on an errand to deliver food to his brothers, he heard this giant threatening the people of God. Incensed by his arrogance, David accepted the challenge of facing him for the honor of the God that he served. Though discouraged by his own brothers and King Saul because of his youth and perceived inexperience, David courageously stood up to the challenges of the giant because he was more angry about Goliath's defiance of God and God's people than he was fearful for his own life. Our courage to face challenges will often be weighed by the consequences of our deference to them. When we realize that if we do not face our challenges they will grow in power against us, then we will find the courage and resolve to stand tall in their midst.

The Courage to Face Confrontation

Men and women who are afraid to face conflict and confrontation are ineffective leaders. They will allow confusion to reign in their midst and will eventually be swallowed up by their fears. Because there will always be obstacles to progress, you must be willing to acknowledge and respond to them properly. Mike Murdoch has said, "You cannot correct what you are unwilling to confront."[3] You also can never change what you will not confront. I heard a man ask his pastor what advice he could share with a female pastor about dealing with difficult people, because she was afraid of confrontation. The advice was, "Tell her to find someone to carry her stick, and appoint and anoint them to do so and let them have their way."

The pastor giving the advice had done just that. He too did not like confrontation, so he had chosen a woman to deal with anything that appeared problematic or uncomfortable to him. Subsequently the power and authority of his church rested in the hands of that woman. The pastor was not respected because it appeared as if he stood for nothing and that he had allowed a woman, who did not have his knowledge of Scripture or his love of God's people, to reign over them. The congregation held the woman with the power and authority in contempt and disdain because most felt she was out of place in saying and doing much of what she did. She had no spiritual credentials or people skills. She simply appeared to be a bully, and many wondered why the pastor allowed her to be so. What they did not understand is that she had been chosen to handle all confrontation.

This example is not uncommon and is usually seen when leaders have been chosen by others and have never made the decision themselves to lead. Sometimes because of their charisma or natural abilities, such leaders have been surrounded by people and encouraged by popular demand to lead. They have looked at the rewards for being in front of the pack—a pack that appeared to be pushing them—and have felt it easy to simply maintain a trot that keeps them in front of the others. Skipping up front has been the extent of their leadership skill, but they have found themselves skipping in place without movement or advancement because they really do not have the inner fortitude to lead the way.

I believe that one of the reasons some cower from confrontation is that they feel it has to be nasty and end up bloody. It most certainly does not. On a personal level, confrontation is good and healthy. In dealing with people one on one, it speaks to one's ability to be assertive without being aggressive and to properly deal with issues or solve problems before they get out of hand. It displays esteem for self and for others. It is a demonstration of strength, sometimes a quiet one, without the need for yelling or exercising bravado.

Vivian Hughes is an example of an African American woman with quiet strength. I have watched her use a creative manner in managing conflict as she works to develop young children. She is first of all a soft-spoken woman, but this is not to be misunderstood as her being a weak one. Hughes is fiercely dedicated to developing and educating children. In 1997 she founded the sign language ensemble Heavenly Hands, a marvelous ministry to the hearing impaired and others. She so beautifully brings inspirational music to life through signing and movement.

However, she has had to face confrontation on many occasions within her church environment because of her work. Through persistence and a soft, though steel, resolve Vivian remains flexible; she may change the manner in which she works, but she never stops it. She holds onto her goal of educating her children and refuses to allow criticism or challenges to deter her. Her efforts are rewarded through the dedication of some fifty sign language students, ages eight and up, whom she teaches discipline, stage presence and self-esteem. Each year they have a major concert, and at the end of it she gives every child a five-hundred-dollar savings bond for college. In the past six years she has given out more than sixty thousand dollars in bonds for college tuition.

TAKING CHARGE VERSUS TAKING OVER

My sister Helen is a principal in Fort Worth, Texas, and has been for many years. She is a very good one; her leadership has been acknowledged through numerous commendations and awards. However, she and I have differed on leadership styles as I have tried unsuccessfully to encourage her to be more assertive outside her school environment. She responded to me one day in this manner: "You see the difference in us is this: I am a take-charge person and you are a take-over person. When given authority I take charge and lead. You don't feel the need to wait until something is given you and you just take over." I still laugh at that description, but I did think seriously on it so that I could modify my approach to leadership. I was much younger and did not have the wisdom that came through the hard-knocks education I would later experience. However, as I said to her then, I still believe that there are times when we must take over because we will never be given permission to take charge. The courage to lead means that you will not do so by permission only.

THE COURAGE TO BE FIRST

There are many situations in which we will desire to lead, but not only will we not be given permission, we also will be discouraged from even thinking about it. Because of economics, or racism and discrimination, there are still many things that African Americans have yet been given the opportunity to do. We are often reading about women and men who are breaking barriers and glass ceilings to forge new paths for African Americans and other minorities. There is a demand for pioneers, and we must have the courage to be first. We tend to applaud those who make history as the first to do many things, but rarely do we think about the enormous sacrifice, courage and discipline that have gone into accomplishing that feat. When one breaks new ground, it is often without role models, mentors and examples that they are able to follow. It has rather been their sheer determination, drive and courage that have goaded them to achieve. It is in having the courage to be a pioneer that true leadership is demonstrated.

Beverly Hannah Jones is the founder and CEO of Hannah & Associates, an architectural and interior-design firm in Michigan. She is one of only five African American women architects in the country who have founded and head their own companies. She also is the only licensed African American female architect with her own firm in the Midwest. In May 1995, *Detroit Monthly* magazine profiled her as an "architect extraordinaire."[4] She admitted to me recently that being in a white male-dominated profession is taxing and it often takes a toll on her enthusiasm for her work. But Jones continues to shine as a clear example of the reward of being dedicated to excellence and of willingness to make the personal sacrifice to achieve.

Valerie Daniels-Carter acknowledges that she faced barriers that hadn't been broken by an African American woman when she opened her first Burger King restaurant in Milwaukee over twenty years ago. Today she runs a 95-million-dollar fast-food empire, and her company, V&J Foods, now owns 140 Burger King and Pizza Hut restaurants in six states. V&J Foods has consistently ranked high on the list of *Black Enterprise* magazine's top 100 list of the largest black-owned businesses in the country. In 2000, the magazine named her one of the "powerhouses of the new economy." Daniels-Carter at-

tributes her success to faith, determination and the ability to overcome hurdles. "All of my strength comes from my faith in God," she
states. "I have a strong foundation in Christianity. It gives me the
strength and the courage that I need to manage from day to day."[5]

Referred to by her minister as "a modern-day Deborah," the Hon-
orable Janice Rogers Brown also relies on faith to sustain her in an often difficult and challenging position as a jurist in the California Su-
preme Court. As the first African American woman appointed to the
court, Brown had to overcome many obstacles before traveling her
pioneer path, among them restrictive racist practices in Alabama,
where she was raised, as well as the prejudicial thinking of her own
family toward lawyers. When Brown declared at a young age that she
wanted to be a lawyer, her family did not meet it with enthusiasm.
She said that she was eight or nine years old before she realized that
"shyster lawyer" was two words. But encouraged by her grand-
mother, who taught her "whatever you do, do it with all your might,"
Brown is now looked upon as "a new paradigm for the west coast political establishment."[6]

THE COURAGE TO CHANGE

Most people fear change not only because it speaks to the unknown
but also because it represents something that we cannot control. It is
this fear that will keep us working for twenty years for someone else
when we know we have the smarts, talent and skill to develop our
own business and to work for ourselves. The fear of change has kept
women in abusive marriages and relationships until their self-esteem
is damaged, many times beyond repair.

A friend said to me recently that whereas he missed my being in
the denomination of my youth, he had to admire my courage to leave
it. He said, "The fact that you could walk away from something that

you had known for all of your life is amazing and I know that it took courage." It did indeed, and I was able to do it only because I considered it a necessary step for me to take in order to survive. It took three years before I got to the point where I had the courage to make that change, but I knew I would never know the promise or potential that God had placed in me until I courageously—and blindly, I might add—walked in the direction of where he wanted me to go.

God has a promise for each of us and we must have the courage to pursue it. Yet there will always be a giant in our promise: some obstacle that seems formidable and some challenge that we must overcome. But we must realize that those giants are figments of our thoughts and imaginations, formulated through the spirit of fear. You are the true giant in your promise because you have the ability to stand in the face of conflict and forge resolution. You are well able to rise above your dark past because you have had a glimpse of your bright future. For your vision of tomorrow can carry you beyond your circumstances today. You are well able to withstand the criticism of those who may never understand who you are and what your purpose is in life. You can endure adversity, confront your adversaries and overcome all obstacles in your way. There are two spirits that desire to encase you. You must choose the spirit of courage, or the spirit of fear will choose you. You must choose to have the courage to be called and chosen so that you may lead—often as a pioneer in areas where the fearful do not walk and where the less talented cannot go.

We need you, black woman, to courageously stand as a beacon of light in a world where darkness rules. We need you, black woman, to courageously stand as a solitary voice for what is right, even among the clamor of those who shout only for what is popular and what is comfortable. We need you to courageously stand because you do understand, as did Henry Ward Beecher, that "greatness comes not in being strong but in the right use of strength." We need you to call upon your ancestral strength and evoke the spirit of the women who withstood the slave ships and the cotton fields, the water hoses and the horses so that you might stand today. It is now our chance to make our choice to lead with courage and we must do so . . . because we can.

QUESTIONS FOR REFLECTION AND DISCUSSION

1. Have you ever been afraid of advancement or promotion for fear of the responsibility and visibility it would bring? How did that fear affect you, or how is it still affecting you?
2. In what ways are you proactively feeding your faith?
3. How beneficial would it be to you to have associates who would also be pregnant with a call of God? Where might you find them?
4. What steps can you take or what things can you do to build your courage and strengthen your leadership?
5. Do you have the courage to be a pioneer?

5   LISTENING TO YOUR CONSCIENCE

We want the truth without compromise.

*W*all Street and corporate America have fallen into moral decline. With the scandals of Enron, WorldCom and other corporations, indictments of their CEOs and rumors of insider trading, we have come to expect that there is little that is ethical about those who would lead our major corporations. They focus more on making huge profits for themselves and their stockholders, and they break business and financial laws to do so. President George W. Bush even called for prison terms for executives who falsify financial statements, appealing to capitalists' self-interest as well as their consciences in an attempt to curtail corporate fraud.[1] At the same time, the church world has been reeling with scandals that involve the betrayal of trust and sexual impropriety among priests and pastors. Though the national spotlight recently has focused primarily on the Catholic Church, there were many instances in which Christian leaders of other denominations fell beneath the standards of acceptable behavior for men and women in the entrusted place of spiritual leadership. These disappointing times have reminded me of a prayer quoted by Dr. Martin Luther King Jr.:

> God give us leaders!
> A time like this demands strong minds, great hearts,
> true faith and ready hands;
> Leaders whom the lust of the office does not kill;
> Leaders whom the spoils of life cannot buy;

Leaders who possess opinions and a will;
Leaders who have honor; leaders who will not lie;
Leaders who can stand before a demagogue
and damn his treacherous flatteries without winking!
Tall leaders, sun crowned, who live above the fog
in public duty and private thinking.[2]

The Motive to Lead

The drive that catapults many into leadership is often something other than a desire to serve. Many times it is the desire to be served by others. This determines the kind of leader one will become. When assuming a leadership role, it is imperative to ask yourself what your true motive is. What we see in our churches, schools, government and on Wall Street today are men and women (though mostly men) whose goals for leading others is secondary to what is desired for self. Their drive is to succeed but not always to lead. Therefore we have leaders who choose to succeed at the expense of others rather than to be leaders who expand the lives of others.

Even though we have been created for leadership and to walk in authority, the proclivity for us is to follow others. There are far more of us who sit in the contentment of being told to do something than there are those willing to stand to give the command as to what to do. Often times this draws men and women who will take advantage of the lack of will or discernment and the trusting spirits of those who follow. Nowhere is this more common and more abused than in our church pulpits. The motive for leadership here is not always integral to the spiritual needs of the parishioners.

Women are commonly victimized by men who twist Scriptures so that the women are held in positions of submission and weakness. When a woman questions such teaching, she is made to feel sinful and disobedient to God and his mandates for her life. Guilt is even placed upon her when she refuses illicit sexual advances from her spiritual leader, to whom she has gone in a vulnerable state, seeking counsel. Unfortunately, because she is more willing to follow than to lead, or because she has been conditioned to believe that she cannot lead, she acquiesces to this emotional abuse. This is, in part, because she does not study the Word of God or seek him for herself.

At the same time, some female leaders are just as abusive. They use their position of spiritual authority to demand treatment and favors from their parishioners—mostly the men—in ways that have little or no connection to biblical teachings. This is simply to ensure that they will be kept on a pedestal and treated as if they are every male member's mate. I have been told about some who require flowers and expensive gifts for Valentine's Day, their birthday and other holidays, without regard to or interest in what those same men might or should be doing for their own wives. I have heard of members sacrificing to ensure that their female pastor has a regal lifestyle that they do not know for themselves or their own families. And they are berated at the slightest resistance to making those sacrifices.

Defined by Character

We have allowed popularity, money and earning power to serve as what defines one's ability to lead. We have used financial standing as a barometer to measure the successful leader. Therefore, by this measurement the best preachers are those who have the largest budgets and offerings, who own the most cars and who surround themselves with the trappings of the corporate executive's success: private planes, helicopters, expensive cars and homes protected by a cadre of security. Those in this position preach but do not pastor; they may pray *for* others but will rarely pray *with* them. They preach tithing and do not tithe themselves. They talk healing but will not go to the hospital for visitation. They have created an aura of power and holiness and have made the flock feel that because of who they are, God has blessed them above others. And they teach that the blessing and provision of God is contingent on one's continuously giving to them, their visiting pastor friends and their vision. Rarely, if ever, do you see these leaders giving money to their people and to anyone outside their private circles. It is a shearing of the flock that is unethical at best, and treacherously deceptive. The very place where character is expected most, it is missing, and churches, as well as our communities, suffer greatly as a result.

> NEARLY ALL MEN CAN STAND ADVERSITY.
> BUT IF YOU WANT TO TEST A MAN'S CHARACTER, GIVE HIM POWER.
>
> **Abraham Lincoln**

Character is not something that anyone can give you. It is not inborn or inherited, neither is it received by associating with others. Rather it is developed through consistent actions and choices based on deeply held beliefs. You cannot hide your character, for when pressed, it seeps through and into your speech and your response to difficulty and crisis. It is your greatest asset and it determines who you really are.

Driven by Character

Two things happen when leaders are driven by character. First, they cannot be corrupted by outside influences. They make decisions based on their consciences and not just in response to reason, for it has been said that reason often makes mistakes, but conscience never does. Leaders driven by integrity and character do what is right simply because it is the right thing to do. They recognize that doing right may not be popular, but it will always be right. It might be costly, but it will be rewarding. Rosa Parks said, "Leadership is often exhibited by one making the right decision at the right time, especially if it is an unpopular one." The negative things going on outside a character-driven leader will never matter to her because she knows they are minimized by what is going on inside her. No matter what is happening around us, we can escape it through some means or measure. But there is no escaping one's conscience, and it is that which must be consulted when making decisions that will impact the lives of others.

The second thing that happens when leaders are driven by character is that they earn the loyalty of those they lead. I have had the privilege of phone conversations with a man who I had never seen or met before he called me some months ago. We both knew that our coming together via the telephone was a God-led occurrence. As we spoke, sometimes in lengthy conversations over the months, we shared with one another some of our personal and professional experiences, and I have been both impressed and touched by the honesty and integrity of this man. Warren Heard is someone who the world may never know, but who everyone would enjoy meeting. He and his family are unusual people and an exhilarating breath of fresh air. As a leader and business owner, he has worn his Christianity above his titles, and through humility and integrity he has been an example of true leadership.

Twenty years ago, Heard founded a healthcare agency in Oklahoma to fill the demand in hospitals due to the shortage of nurses. One hospital in particular noticed that the nurses he sent were not only outstanding in their skills but also were different in their demeanor and approach to their work. The hospital hired more and more of them until one day the board of directors noticed that a very large percentage of their nursing staff came from that single agency. They decided it was not in their best interest to be so dependent on an outside entity, and they decided to end the relationship with the agency. The administration served notice to Heard that by the end of the next week the hospital would no longer use his services.

This was a devastating blow to Heard's agency because he was responsible for the employment of all of those nurses and knew that it would be impossible to reassign them elsewhere in a week's time. The hospital then decided they would offer to hire his nurses directly if any of them wanted to work on the staff instead of with Heard. The hospital came up with a rather sweet deal for the nurses, offering them the choice of their working assignments and a 33-percent raise. Heard released his nurses from their contracts with him and encouraged them to consider their own needs and take the hospital's offer. He knew it would take time for him to develop a plan to keep them working, and he didn't want them to be without during that time. However, 100 percent of the nurses voted singly and independently to remain with his agency. One by one they said they would wait in faith to see what Heard could do to find them employment elsewhere. Their loyalty shocked the hospital administration. Not a single nurse accepted their offer, honoring the faith and integrity of the man they called their leader.

THE INFLUENCE OF MONEY

The influence of money on leadership is seen in every aspect of life: politics, religion, education, business, sports, entertainment, media, civic and community arenas. Money is important to the successful running of programs and is needed to do good things and especially to do them well. All too often schools, ministries and other non-profit organizations are forced to spend too much time and energy in fundraising just to carry out the vision they have to help those they serve. This brings frustration that leads people to receive funding that is not always in the best interest of their organizations.

There also are outside forces that would simply use money and its influence to persuade leaders in ways that would weaken the vision and the goals of their organization and diminish its impact. In politics this is legal, and it is called lobbying. In business and even medicine, it is done through vendors, whose sole responsibility is to influence those in decision-making positions to use them or their products over others. Often the needs of patients become secondary to the doctor's commitment to a particular company or business. Money has prejudiced our thinking and persuaded us to abandon lofty goals and idealistic thinking in exchange for the average way of doing business as usual.

In 1993 columnist Bob Herbert decried the willingness of African American leaders and organizations to trade health and wholeness for money from the tobacco industry. Smoking is a danger and a terrible habit for anyone, but it seems to be an awful plague within the African American community in particular. We die by the thousands from cancer and smoking-related diseases. Herbert felt that our leaders should have been fanatical in their opposition to smoking. Instead they lost their voice and became silently absent in the fight against this injury, because tobacco companies had poured millions into the coffers of our political and community leaders and their organizations.[3] The same can be said about the liquor industry, whose contributions often support black causes. In many ways we have seen our need for money become our greed for money, and at times a good intention turned into a bad invention because of it.

I remember years ago being so impressed with a woman from the Detroit area whom I saw on *The Oprah Winfrey Show*. Named by the cosmetics company Avon as one of six Women of Enterprise in the nation, she was hailed as an outstanding businesswoman who had turned a personal tragedy into a multimillion-dollar educational and daycare headquarters for hundreds of children in the metropolitan Detroit area. Marie Jackson-Randolph was featured in books and articles about successful, enterprising women and was highly regarded for her massive accomplishments in life.

In 1979 Jackson-Randolph survived a fire in her home that took the lives of her three children. She overcame this tremendous disaster and forged a path for herself that would be daunting and even impossible to anyone less determined and focused. Jackson-Randolph became a lawyer, college professor, member of the Detroit Public School board, and founder, president and CEO of MAJCO Inc., which had sixteen daycare centers and a school of achievement. Through her Sleepy Hollow Educational Centers, she established the largest black-owned daycare chain in the nation.

However, the government said that from 1988 to 1993 Jackson-Randolph and her food-program coordinator had defrauded the U.S. Agriculture Department's Child Care Food Program of 15.5 million dollars by filing false claims. In June 1999, a jury found her guilty on all sixty-three counts, and she was sentenced to nine years in prison.[4] Her fall from grace was sad and seemed unbelievable, but even more shocking was the greed and lavish lifestyle that contributed to her decisions to misuse money designated to feed poor children. When the U.S. marshals went to seize property from the home of Jackson-Randolph, among other things they found 911 purses, 606 pairs of shoes, nearly 350 furs, 165 pairs of boots, and enough china and crystal to host a state dinner. An entire room in her exclusive Palmer Woods home—from floor to ceiling—was devoted to costume jewelry. One U.S. assistant attorney described the excess as obscene.[5]

In 1903 W. E. B. Du Bois wrote, "In the Black World, the Preacher and Teacher embodied once the ideals of this people—the strife for another and a juster world, the vague dream of righteousness, the mystery of knowing; but today the danger is that these ideals, with their simple beauty and weird inspiration, will suddenly sink to a question of cash and a lust for gold."[6] We can ill afford to lose our leaders to a lust for money and things, because we lose more than individuals when it occurs. When silence is exchanged for money, we fail to speak to the needs of our community, and our communities eventually become deaf to our cries for change and advancement. When the poor and illiterate see the few educated and endowed turn their backs on them or sell them to the highest bidder, they respond in ways that become deadly to more of us. They drop out of the political process and do not vote, leaving our communities helpless to politicians who will not speak to their needs. They lose interest in worshiping and become deaf to the words of those who would encourage making choices for education and moral living that would decrease their poverty and increase their hopes. Their heroes and role models become the drug dealers who at least live in their communities and who appear to be giving them something, though they too are robbing them of their future and their dreams.

The African American community must raise within itself a higher level of leadership, and women, it must begin with us. If anybody can withstand the lure of quick money, we can. It is common to us to take little and do much with it. We have learned through necessity how to raise our children without assistance and to nurture them to greatness on a shoestring budget, with great faith and prayer. We educated our children at the finest colleges and universities by washing and ironing clothes and cleaning toilets. The myth of the welfare queen being a black able-bodied woman who just won't work is just that, a myth. Few have worked harder and longer than we and with as little resources accomplished as much. We have what it takes to stand on what is right just because it's right and to make the choices that reflect our consciences. We cannot afford to ignore what we know is right for us and this entire country simply because we don't want to hurt someone's feeling or stir up the pot. The pot has been stirred for years with toxins that are slowly killing us, and we have the recipe that will provide us a more healthy serving of food.

LISTEN TO YOUR CONSCIENCE

It is commonly understood that women have that special *something* within them: the warning system we call women's intuition, which helps us to make wise decisions and to avoid trouble. As we assume positions of leadership, we need not feel that we should abandon the gifts that we have as women. Someone has said, "Those who ignore their conscience forsake their best friend and lifetime guide." We need to use our intuition and discretion, and listen to our consciences as a leading force in our decision-making process. We must hear ourselves above the din of the noisome voices that would have us settle for less than we should by encouraging us toward decisions that would make us wealthy and independent of those we serve.

It is a rare sight, though a welcome one, when a political representative in Congress or the Senate goes against popular opinion to vote the way of conscience. It is something I applaud even when I disagree with the opinion that he or she represents. I appreciate the courage displayed in standing for something one believes in.

Our guide for leadership must come from something other than our personal needs and our desire to establish our next career move. We must have the fortitude to lead by our conscience; to speak to the needs of our community; to stand on the pillars of integrity and, even in the face of struggle, to refuse to take money that will buy our si-

lence. It is past time that we address those things that we have come
to accept: out-of-wedlock births that weaken our families and keep
us in poverty; illiteracy among our teens and adults; men who do not
face the responsibilities that should come with the sexual favors that
we too willingly offer; images that we have created in print, television, music and movies that defame us and keep us struggling with
our self-esteem. In 1998, then-retired General Colin Powell said, "We
have got to restore a sense of shame."[7] He was addressing the need to
reduce out-of-wedlock pregnancies, but we can apply it to so much
more. There was a time when we just didn't do certain things because
of what we had been taught and what we saw in our homes and
neighborhoods. However, as we turned our eyes beyond our imme-
diate surroundings, the paradigm for what is proper and suitable behavior changed, and we did not resist it. We are like frogs that jump
around in the pot of cold water on a stove. We notice that the heat in
it is slightly increasing, yet we adjust to the heat until it cooks us, instead of jumping out of the pot to save our lives.

LEAD BY EXAMPLE

Mahatma Gandhi said, "We must be the change we want to see in the
world." We must not ask others to do for us what we are unwilling to
do for ourselves. We must lead by example and demand the same
from those who would lead us. It is not about putting people on a
pedestal either. It is about being what you would ask someone else to
stretch to become. It is about accepting the responsibility for the
rights you enjoy. When thirty-year-old Kwame Kilpatrick was cam-
paigning to become the youngest mayor in the history of Detroit, he
would talk about how he grew up in a home where involvement in
public service was second nature and expected. He would quote his
mother, Congresswoman Carolyn Cheeks-Kilpatrick, as having

taught him that "public service is the rent you pay for the space that you occupy." He had been made to believe that he had a responsibility to society simply because he lived.

There was talk about the musicians, actors and actresses who came together to raise money for the victims of the September 11 tragedies. They got on television and asked everyday working Americans to give their best financial effort to support the families left behind by the loss of life at the Trade Center, at the Pentagon and in Pennsylvania. But many of them, who are wealthy and who live very comfortably, if not lavishly, did not make the sacrifice that they were asking of others. These are those that we have chosen as leaders and role models for ourselves and our children, and they prove to us continuously that they do not deserve such a place with us and should not be given the privilege or responsibility of influence.

Can we as African American women be trusted to lead? Will our character and integrity be reflected in what we do in the stress of the storm and in the calm of the aftermath? Can we give our word and keep our word? I say yes, because we have witnessed the eating away of the moral fiber of society for too long. I say yes, because we have seen the destruction of our families, schools and churches by those who lack our skills for leadership and our altruistic desire for what is in the best interest of us all. Leadership is a position of honor and it should be approached as such. There is a demand for credibility in us and among those who lead us. We have that internal anchor that would keep us grounded in what is right, even when our ship turns wrong. We have the strength to dig deep and to hold on to what our conscience tells us is the way we should go. We should become the next generation of leaders who are driven by the call of our consciences.

QUESTIONS FOR REFLECTION AND DISCUSSION

1. Evaluate your motives for leadership.
2. How do you define character and in what ways is it demonstrated in your life as a leader?
3. Reflect on the influence of money in your community, city and church, and its impact on the decisions of the leaders.
4. What changes might occur if we had conscience-driven leadership?

6 MAINTAINING YOUR COMMITMENT

With swollen ankles and tired feet
You never thought to take a seat.

When you look at the leaders who have demonstrated a commitment to impacting the world, they are always people who could have very easily succeeded at something else—something less demanding of them and something that could have brought them more personal gain. They did not sacrifice themselves and their lives by force, but by choice. I have often looked upon Martin Luther King Jr. with profound respect and admiration because of the single choice that he made to live his life in service to humanity. Though born black in America during times when racism and hatred for African Americans ruled, he was a middle-class man who had been educated at the best schools. His intelligence and background could have allowed him to live well above the less-than-average means that was afforded to other blacks. He could have been content to be among the accepted few and to enjoy the privilege that came with it. But King realized that what God gave him wasn't just for him and it wasn't about him; it was all for others. This is the vital lesson we must learn to be committed leaders. We must see ourselves as the vessels through which God can reach the world. We must see our resources as tools for others and not just reservoirs for ourselves.

It appears that the word *commitment* either is not used much today or has actually changed in meaning. Do you find people to be as dedicated as they used to be? In many cases it is difficult to find those who would do anything consistently, much less in the model of devotion. There are some things that we do passionately for a brief period, but the passion quickly wanes and dissipates, and we are back to the nonchalant manner in which we seem to do most things. Our focus is different now, and we appear to be easily distracted.

In some ways technology has brought this about. We are in a microwave society where things change so quickly and we have access to so much that we are no longer willing to demonstrate patience in waiting on things or people to develop. We lose our interest very quickly. I wonder if prosperity has done this to us, for ease in living can give us a false sense of security and cause us to feel detached from the people and things that once held our dearest attention. This argument can definitely be made in regard to African Americans. There used to be things that we did with fervor because we believed them to be essential to our survival. We fought for causes and rallied in support of things that we felt threatened us and our future. During the early civil rights movement we displayed a fiery dedication to end segregation laws and to demand equal rights. We marched in the rain and withstood water hoses, dogs and horses that were used to plow through our heart-linked lines in an attempt to stop us. And nothing could! For more than a year, we walked in Montgomery, Alabama, pooled together resources of both people and money, and stood defiantly instead of sitting in the back of segregated buses, until the Jim Crow laws were dismantled before us. We walked for fifty miles from Selma to Montgomery, endured Bloody Sunday and refused to be turned in our march to secure voting rights in the state of Alabama. Over and over in other cities and states the cries of our oppression were met with collective action because we cared so deeply and wanted so badly to be free. But with the comfort of entering doors not marked "colored only" and the relative ease of our movement throughout the country, we have become dispassionate about the needs that yet remain, and we have turned our heads and closed our eyes to sacrificial involvement. David L. Evans, admissions adviser at Harvard University, has spoken to the issue that those who benefited from the civil rights movement are not participating in its continuance. He has questioned the whereabouts of activists that are fifty and younger and has challenged them to take leaves of absences from their jobs to work a year or two for civil and human-rights groups. He said, "Leadership shouldn't be the lifetime responsibility of just a handful of men and women." He went on to say that he did not want to suggest that they were "uninformed, self-absorbed ingrates," but, like so many others, he simply wants to understand why it is so hard to get them involved in the struggle.[1] It might just be because it no longer is a struggle, and comfort tends to lessen the desire of a man or woman to fight.

This is not the case for all people, and it was proven to us on September 11, 2001. In the worst possible way America got a picture of what it means to be committed. For at the core of the religious zeal and hatred that seemed to drive the men who hijacked the airplanes and flew them to their murderous acts, there was a level of commitment unmatched by any we had seen in our lifetime. Some would think that these men had been convinced through brainwashing to sacrifice their lives for their terror cell and its evil leader. But in looking into the backgrounds of those men, a different picture is revealed, and it is far more disturbing than that. The story that unfolds is hard to understand from an intellectual stance because these were intelligent, educated, middle-class young men. They had everything to gain and could have accomplished a great deal in the opportunity-filled country they had come to hate. But unlike so many in this country, they were not driven by dreams of things that they could possess, but by a passion that possessed them. This passion caused them to demonstrate a commitment over years as they studied to be pilots and learned the intricate details of the plan that they would carry out to an evil perfection. They taught us on that pain-filled day that, for evil or good, a person of commitment cannot be stopped or matched by those who are blasé in their beliefs and in what motivates them toward life.

Why doesn't good drive us to fanaticism? Is there no longer a passion for those who suffer: the poor and the indigent? Is there no cause that could stir us to fight for the underdogs of society and to forcefully lay claim on what we believe is right? We have so labeled people over the years that have been passionate about their beliefs, calling them liberal and painting them as standing to the left of what was *really* right. Then those who stood and professed their love of country differently and their desire for wholesome living were painted as right-wing conservatives. Few wanted to be connected to either of those groups. It has become more popular and acceptable to be a centrist, one who stands somewhere comfortable between the two groups, and most people have flocked to this place. However, the place where there is no paint generally has no passion, and the passionless are not committed to anything other than themselves.

There is a story that Jesus tells about a man who spends his life and time focusing on himself and his desire to hold onto all that he has. He was a blessed man in that his grounds brought forth much fruit. Because he looked upon his blessing as being only for himself, he considered ways to hoard what he had and not to share it. A life of comfort and ease was his desire, and he thought it would make him happy. But God called him a fool, for the very things that he would live for, he died for, and his treasures would be enjoyed by others. Jesus said that the man had accumulated his riches for himself but was not rich toward God. (See Luke 12:16-21.) It is interesting to say one is not rich toward God. Who is more rich than God? He made everything and owns everything. What on earth, literally, could he need? So often we think only in terms of what we give monetarily in churches. But the manner in which God is seen is in and through the work of people. How else is our richness toward God manifested than through what we do for others?

In February 2003 I attended the Tavis Smiley presentation "The State of the Black Union IV/The Black Church: Relevant, Repressive, or Reborn?" It was a powerful exchange between some of the brightest, most respected African American theologians in the country. At one point during the discussion that focused on the need of the country and the church to be more socially conscious, the Reverend Al Sharpton made a comment that complemented my thoughts on being rich toward God. He said that so often we pray and sing for God to bless America when it's really time that America bless God. He said that we bless God when we take care of the poor and indigent. We bless God when we secure our senior citizens. We bless God when we demonstrate compassion to the least of these because, Jesus said, "In as much as ye have done it unto one of the least of these my brethren, ye have done it unto me" (Matthew 25:40). What God needs is for us to yield our resources and ourselves to him so that they and we can be used for the benefit of others.

One Sunday a word of prophecy came forth in a service I was visiting: "God is saying," the woman cried out, "whatever it is that you love about him, he wants to see in you!" Immediately I thought about how much I love and appreciate his faithfulness. It is in this that we see first the difference between him and people. We serve a God of devotion and commitment. He tells us in his Word that he doesn't change and he cannot lie (see Malachi 3:6; Titus 1:2). It is the manner in which he consistently loves and forgives day after day that makes me love him most. But if I am to be likewise faithful, devoted and committed to him, it must be seen in how I regard his people.

COMMIT FIRST TO A PRINCIPLED LIFE

There is no better leadership than that which is grounded in conviction and principles that are mirrored in the everyday life of the one who leads. If one does not display a devotion to faith and hope in humanity, it is not probable that people will have faith or hope in her ability to lead. The best leader leads by example. She says "I will" before she says "you should." Her life speaks of who *she* is before she attempts to mold the identity of another. Before she can lead someone to obtain something, she demonstrates what it is to *be* something. Her life is more about excellence than success. The difference between the two is that success is defined by what you have whereas excellence speaks to who you are. Success can be fleeting, but a person of excellence will bring it about again and again.

A principled life is not one that is shaped only by one's IQ—their level of intelligence—but also by one's "adversity quotient"—a life that is formed by the things that it encounters in the valley. And it is a life called toward those things that are idealistic, high and noble. Few commit to such a life, primarily because it is not necessary anymore. It is not a requirement to be principled to be prosperous. It is not necessary to reaching the pinnacles of success and enjoying the trappings that come with it. It is not much more connected to those who profess Christianity even, because the bar has been lowered in that arena, as in all other areas of life. But the minority who commit themselves to living a life of conviction, value and ethical principles stand far above the rest. Their lives command the respect and loyalty that others demand.

COMMIT TO PRINCIPLED LEADERSHIP

So many people believe leadership simply to be the attainment of
power and the ability to earn money. Yet there are many with power
and money whom we reluctantly refer to as leaders. Pimps have
power. They lord themselves over women and harangue them
through emotional and physical abuse. Drug dealers are often known
to run sophisticated organizations in and out of prisons that exceed
many small corporations. Bullies have power that they have wrestled
from those who they intimidate.

All these and more—some of whom are in legitimate fields—can
be considered to be leaders when we use the definition that a leader
is one who demands the attention and duty of others. Because people
tend to follow those who are stronger than they, this attention and
duty is garnered by those who have neither integrity nor honor in
their dealings. But through force of personality they have demanded
their will to stand over others as leaders.

Principled leaders empower those they lead; they don't enslave
them. Their agenda is transparent and simple: to increase and enrich
the lives of those who follow them. They influence through inspiration, not intimidation. Their companies, organizations and churches
are not built as mere monuments to their egos, but demonstrate from
top to bottom the value of every employee and member. The principled leader does not take the golden parachute, accepting millions of
dollars in buyouts as the company lays off thousands who have to de-
pend on every paycheck just to survive. Morality—not just legality—
is the measurement for their dealings with those they lead.

The Reverend Jim Holley pastors the historic Little Rock Baptist
Church in Detroit. I heard him discuss his role as leader of his flock
recently on the TV program *For My People,* which is taped at his
building. Holley said that leaders, especially ministers, needed to re-

alize that "members are not here for us—we're here for them." He spoke of the importance of preachers not being satisfied to have a standard of living that far exceeds their flock's but should desire that their flock enjoy the privileges they do. To that end his church developed the S.E.E. goal for its members: Salvation, Education and Economics. The desire is to fill the spiritual needs of the church, to see that congregants receive the education they need and to motivate them toward business empowerment and entrepreneurship. To this end, Little Rock runs an extensive adult education program and provides scholarships for college. In addition, their motto is to move members from "ON to OWN." The desire is to move them from being *on* welfare or *on* the payroll of someone else to having something they *own* themselves. In light of the fact that Holley is himself a very successful and prosperous businessman, his attitudes and actions for his church reflect a principled leadership.

Commit to Sacrificial Leadership

There was a time when it was expected that leaders would give up more than their followers because they set the tone and example of what was desired or required for their success as a unit. During the civil rights movement, Martin Luther King Jr., Ralph Abernathy and other leaders slept in the same tents on cold ground as those who joined them in protest. Encouraged to go to nearby hotels to ensure his health and safety, King refused to separate himself from the crowd. He would not ask others to do what he was unwilling to do himself. Sacrificial leadership was the norm for that time and movement. There was always the belief that someone else would benefit, in addition to or perhaps even more than the leader. For sacrificial leadership occurs when people are able to see outside their own needs and use their gifts and abilities to bring the best for those who they may never see or know.

I know that we are busy women with responsibilities of family, career and ministry that keep us long on work and short on time to get it all done. It seems that asking us to sacrifice more is asking for blood, yet there are things that call us forth, that beckon our involvement, that we feel compelled to respond to because of their impact on so many.

In 2002 I read an alarming statistic on illiteracy in the state of Michigan: over 50 percent of the citizens in the city of Detroit are functionally illiterate. Immediately I called to see what I could do and volunteered to teach a man to read. During my training, however, I kept telling myself that I didn't have the time to commit to faithfully carrying out the program. But because I had given my word to the church out of which I would teach, I remained in the program. Upon completion of my first class with my learner, I was so moved by the genuine appreciation from the man, who had cried out for help and waited for more than a year for a tutor, I gave gratitude and thanksgiving to God for the privilege of being the vehicle through which he finally got his help. But it was many months later, when he called to tell me that he had been nominated to become president of his union, that I really was able to see and feel the impact of my sacrifice. What I thought was for just one turned out to benefit so many others, and it raised the self-esteem and confidence of a single man who is now the leader of many.

At the National Voting Rights Museum, located at the foot of the Edmund Pettus Bridge in Selma, Alabama, visitors are told the story of Bloody Sunday and the attempt to walk from Selma to Montgomery to campaign for voting rights. On the day my family visited, the story was told by a woman who participated in that walk. She looked at the children gathered in the room and with great emotion said, "We did this for you and we didn't even know your name." Sacrifice was an accepted part of the struggle in the fight for civil rights. Unfortunately the gains made do not seem to have been met with the appreciation and willingness of others to give of themselves in the same manner. Instead of lending ourselves to the nameless, we lead to make a name for ourselves. Many may not realize that Martin Luther King Jr. had been awarded the Nobel Prize for Peace in Oslo, Norway, before he called for the march from Selma to Montgomery. His name and image were recognized throughout the world, but his involvement in the struggle for human rights was not abated by his fame. He did not know the names of those for whom he marched, but he knew they could not vote.

COMMIT TO PREPARED LEADERSHIP

Regardless of how inspiring and motivating a leader can be, if she is not a prepared leader, her influence will wane and she will eventually lose the respect of the pack. Inspiration and motivation are good. They are necessary but also temporary. You need a plan. It is commitment that leads one into planning, for it speaks to dedication, discipline and focus. The leader may get the attention of the group, but the plan will get and keep them working. The Bible says, "Where there is no vision, the people perish" (Proverbs 29:18). Visionary leadership lends itself to long-term goals that do more than bring about temporary solutions; they usher in radical change. Planned leadership demonstrates strength, and organization gives confidence to any group.

The commitment to planned leadership also means that you will prepare yourself as well as others for whatever may lie ahead. A prepared leader will have a course of action for a project but also a compass for the future. She will be able to determine what she needs to do to meet the demands of the task ahead, and she will make the personal sacrifices to meet those needs.

COMMIT TO PERSEVERE

No one has ever won a race they quit. No one has ever accomplished anything great that they gave up on. No one has ever fulfilled dreams that they walked away from when things became difficult. Success stories are told only by those who persevere. Real leaders don't quit. They don't see the storm coming and secure their place of safety while their people are left to deal with the ramifications of strong winds that have blown misfortune in their faces. Real leaders hold on. They know that though their grip is strained by the demands upon them and that they are often weighed down with unreasonable responsibilities, they don't let go on their people. Real leaders hold out. They cannot be bought out by those who would block their righteous agenda and leave their followers wandering aimlessly. They will never settle for just enough for themselves but will hold out until all have been able to enjoy a piece of the pie. When faced with a closed door, leaders understand that sometimes knocking will get them in, but other times will require a *push*.

P.U.S.H.

Persevere Under Stress and Hostility. It is not realistic for you to expect hands that will applaud your every effort to forcefully bring change to this world. Sometimes you will find those hands around your throat, and the very people that you will work hard and sacrifice for will criticize you and look at you with suspicion and sometimes with disdain. If a position of leadership represents a place of popularity and comfort, it is one wherein little is accomplished and few are respected. To seek such a place is to forgo influence, for influence is measured as much by those who fight against your efforts as it is by those who support them. To give birth to new ideas that would invigorate the imaginations and challenge the traditions and practices of the masses may sometimes require pushing. Success and achievement threaten mediocrity, and those who like mediocrity often respond with hostility. Don't give in to the naysayers behind the door. *Push!*

Persist Until Satisfaction Happens. Determine what it is that you want and be persistent until it occurs. Get on somebody's nerves, if necessary, for a person is considered a pest only when she has gotten somebody's attention. It is important for leaders to be able to say no, but sometimes it is more important that they cannot hear no.

There is a story about a Gentile woman whose daughter was vexed with demons. She went to Jesus and cried out for his help, and he ignored her. The disciples were bothered about her following them and seeking Jesus' help; they wanted to send her away. But this woman would not easily be turned away; she persisted in her worship and her plea to Jesus to help her. Because Jesus had been sent to the Jews, he finally responded to her by saying that it would not be good for him to give what belonged to the Jews to dogs, the common reference to the Gentiles. But because this woman had a need that rose above her knowledge of tradition, culture and practice, she persisted in seeking Jesus to help her. She said, "Yes, Lord, but even the dogs eat the crumbs that fall from their masters' table" (Matthew 15:27 NIV). Impressed by her persistent faith, Jesus gave her what she desired of him. In a like manner we must go against our knowledge of how things have always been done in the past and *push* until we get what we want. Our communities need better police protection, so we must *push*. Our children need better schools, so we must *push*. We are often led by unresponsive city councils, mayors or state representatives that act as if we are gullible and treat us as if we are invisible, so we must *push*. Former U.S. President Calvin Coolidge said, "Nothing in the world can take the place of Persistence. Talent will not;

nothing is more common than unsuccessful men with talent. Genius will not; unrewarded genius is almost a proverb. Education will not; the world is full of educated derelicts. Persistence and Determination alone are omnipotent."

Press Upon Shaky Hopes. It is important to note that any hope we have is shaky if it is rooted in governmental programs or any institutions that we hold dear. We want to believe in our schools, our churches, our government and each other, and to a certain degree we should and we must. But as a foundation for us, they are inconsistent at best. Yet knowing that these things and nothing that this world has to offer can be looked upon as the best foundation on which any of us can build a life, we still must assert these hopes to the length that they will and can withstand our pushing, until we receive the best that they have to offer us. We must press upon all of our hopes and dreams until we bring them to fruition. There is too much at stake to leave them without the imprints of our hands and hearts. We must be like Abraham who "against hope believed in hope" (Romans 4:18) until our promise and vision can be realized. There are times in which we simply must press on. In the face of discouragement and disappointment, we must press on. Until vilification turns into validation, we must press on.

> Press on, press on
> Ever be steadfast, faithful and strong
> Don't rest but do your best
> To just keep on pressing on.[2]

Pull Upon Somebody's Heart. There are many who would choose to discount or dismiss the emotional leader, but I am not among them. You can never overlook the importance of motivation and inspiration for those that follow you. A leader who chooses to intimidate rather than motivate is one who will be limited in her influence among her people as well as in the amount of time that she will serve them. For people will not stay under an intimidating leadership forever. They will leave you and tear you apart once they are gone, or even worse, stay and try to destroy you from within. As we lead, it is imperative that we study and discern the people with whom we come in contact and come to know exactly what it is that drives them. And we would be wise to use those things to motivate them to their highest good. However, we must realize that the greatest inspiration and motivation for any people is the example set by their leader. We can do more for others and get them to do more for us by the manner in which we choose to work, give and live. We can successfully pull on somebody's heart when they see first that we have one.

Pray Until Something Happens. There is a parable taught by Jesus to his disciples about a woman who goes to see an unjust judge. This judge does not fear God or have regard for people. But the woman is persistent in asking that he avenge her, and he does so because of her insistence that she be heard. He didn't respond to her because she had rights; in the early Jewish culture, a woman had none. But she needed a situation changed in her life and in this model for prayer she sought the help of the judge with fervor and consistency. He didn't hear her case because he thought God would condemn him if he did otherwise. Because of his disregard for people, he was not compelled to be "politically correct." But the judge knew one thing: that woman was going to worry him to death, and for her persistence alone he responded to her need. (See Luke 18:1-5.) As an introduction to this parable Jesus tells his disciples and apostles, "Men ought always to pray, and not to faint" (Luke 18:1). "Not to faint" means never to quit. In other teachings he said, "Keep on asking and it shall be given you" (Matthew 7:7 AMP). It is clear that God wants us to be persistent in prayer. We need to pray because prayer changes people and people can change things. We need to pray because doing so acknowledges that God is the Source of all that we have and all that we need. We need to pray with persistence because it demonstrates our faith in God's promise to hear us and to answer our prayers.

We must commit ourselves to persistence, perseverance, pulling, pressing, pushing and prayer because with so much and so many depending on us, we do not have the luxury of a passive or placid demeanor. We must commit to leadership that will make a difference and bring significant change. And as committed leaders we must sometimes push past those who would deter our efforts to bring about that needed change, because it is the right thing to do, it is the best thing to do and we are the ones who can do it.

QUESTIONS FOR REFLECTION AND DISCUSSION

1. How did commitment shape our leaders of the past and to what level does it do so today?
2. How would you define or describe a principled leader? Consider the examples of those around or before you.
3. What things can you commit to that would make you a more effective leader?
4. In what ways can you *push* to bring about change for those you serve?

7 DEVELOPING COMPASSION

You've been the one to clear the way
For others to travel day by day.

$\mathcal{U}$nfortunately it appears that when compassion is needed most in our country, it is seen the least in our leadership. We seem to have fewer programs now than ever before that demonstrate compassion for the less fortunate and the downtrodden. In our attempt to reform social programs to make all citizens more responsible and less dependent on the government, we have often shut down those agendas that would attempt to bring a level plane for the disenfranchised and those who through birth or bad breaks have not been able to take full advantage of the opportunities of this rich nation. It is interesting that during any election year, we tend to paint a negative view of those candidates and leaders who would even speak to any issue of compassionate reform. Subsequently we have hungry people in a world where more than enough food exists to feed anybody who should desire to eat. And we have over a half-million homeless men, women and children in America, many of whom hold jobs but are simply too poor to have homes. And although there are advocates that exist for each of these groups and others of merit, there seems to be a silence among our national leaders, who all too often are influenced by the desires of those who have rather than moved by the needs of those who have not.

There have been times when compassion has been looked on as a weakness in those who lead us. I well remember the discussions held as to whether Jimmy Carter could be a good President, because many feared that his professed Christianity would make him too soft a leader for our country. We tend to favor those people who are more prone to war than peace and who do less for the masses. To do less, we believe, means that we will have a more streamlined government and that translates as efficiency, which of course ultimately means fewer taxes. However, this is a method of mathematics that always seems to subtract the poor from our policies, adds to the coffers of the wealthy and keeps us all divided. Is there no place anymore for compassion in our local, state and national governments? Have we taken the heart out of leadership? Is there really no balm in Gilead?

Some would argue, and have done so successfully, that acts of compassion should be left only to charities and churches. But over the years we have seen even fewer churches provide programs or outreach ministries to address the needs of the widows and orphans— the two groups they are scripturally charged to cover. With the exception of Christmas and Thanksgiving holidays, many have no programs that are benevolent and demonstrate a heartfelt response to the needy. It has been interesting to watch churches scurry to develop agendas to fit the Faith-Based and Community Initiative requirements that the Bush administration has established to provide money to those churches, ministries and others that would assist others, thus bringing relief to the demands upon the government. But some of these programs in the African American church are focused on money, not on needs, and therefore will not do what old-fashioned compassionate giving and living used to do in years past. For there was a time when in our community the church served as the very heartbeat of the village. It was there that we were kept informed about any and all issues that would affect us. The church was a source of education, communication and, of course, inspiration. But we also knew that if there was a single place where we could find compassionate leadership, it was also there.

JESUS WAS MOVED WITH COMPASSION

Economic development and financial independence have been the focus of the black church in the twenty-first century. We have been called to become business owners and encouraged toward being producers more than consumers. For years we have seen the need to control those business entities within our own communities so that we can keep strong and vital neighborhoods and schools. We have not always been successful at this; it appears that black churches, hair salons and funeral homes are the only things we can point to that are consistently financially successful in our communities. So the messages of economic development and debt management are needed from the pulpit because that is still the best platform for educating us. But when these messages are absent of examples of compassion and benevolence, they do not serve our communities well. We must be called to compassionate leadership within this country, and the black community in particular. We can never afford to turn our churches solely into business institutes given over to teachings and attitudes that exhibit a hardness of heart toward the less fortunate simply because some of us have "arrived."

Despite the great advancement we have come to know, our needs for each other are still too great, and they will always be. The greatest response to our needs should come from us, not from a group outside the black community. We have been criticized on the international front because of our lack of commitment to the needs of our motherland. As we enjoy the freedom and financial opportunities of this great nation, we have not been driven by a heart toward the poverty of our brothers and sisters in Africa. We have not done as the Jews or other immigrant groups who, with consistency and in great measure, send money and resources back to their homelands. Thus we have remained disconnected to their struggle and primarily focused on our own.

But even our own struggle seems to consume us to the point of selfishness, and we have not always been willing to share what we have with each other so that more will have and less will need. It is unfortunate and difficult to accept that this attitude permeates our churches, for our greatest example of leadership is our compassionate Christ. Within the Gospels we read where he was "moved with compassion" toward the multitudes (Matthew 14:14; Mark 6:34).

The Reverend Mother Jessica Kendall Ingram sets a different, compassionate example. Through the Fifteenth Episcopal District Women's Missionary Society of the African Methodist Episcopal Church, Ingram is building the Balm in Gilead Center: The Healing Place for Women in Wallacedene, South Africa. This building and project is the vision of Ingram. In addition to raising the needed funds, she personally oversees the construction of the center, which will serve as a health and education facility to the women in the impoverished area of Wallacedene.

Because women are given to nurturing, to healing pain and to empathy, we are well suited to leadership of charities, missions and ministries with compassionate agendas. And in most cases we do so very well. Therefore a call to lead with compassion comes automatically to us with the expectation that we can and will rise to the demand to govern with care and kindness. For African American women not to lead with compassion is to betray our history. It is to close our eyes to the sacrifices of our ancestors and therefore limit the vision of our future.

Do Something

Charleszetta "Mother" Waddles was the consummate compassionate leader. A humble woman and mother of ten, she still found room to love and care for children who were not her own. These "children" were often adults who were homeless, hungry, naked and addicted. She became mother to them because she turned no one away and lovingly taught, chided and encouraged each one to turn from hopeless living to a faith in God and themselves. Loving was a life passion for her, and she was known for her tireless work among the poor on Detroit's skid row. Often she worked under the threat of her utilities being shut off because her money didn't match her love, but both were eclipsed by a persistence to do what she felt God placed her on earth to do. "We're trying to show what the church could mean to the world if it lived by what it preached," Mother Waddles told *Newsweek*. "I read the Bible. It didn't say just go to church. It said, 'Do something.'"[1]

For eighty-eight years she did something, and upon her death nothing was more telling about the depth of her life's donation and the quality of her quiet leadership than the throngs of the poor and downtrodden who mingled with city and state officials, with the rich and elite to say goodbye to this warrior for the weak. When she lay in state, there was a line of us waiting to respectfully view her remains. As I was about to approach the casket, two men came in holding up a thin, sick young woman. From their appearances, the three of them seemed to fit the profile of her "children," and they were deeply moved by the moment. They held up the frail woman as she leaned over to kiss Mother Waddles goodbye. She then told them to take pictures of her with "Mama" one last time, because that was the woman who had saved her life. Though named to the Michigan Women's Hall of Fame, written about in major national magazines, given multiple citations by everyone from businesses to presidents, and even covered in a documentary by PBS, Mother Waddles never changed. She was never impressed by those who were impressed by her, and with diligence she stayed committed to the charge that she got from reading the Word of God. She did something.

YOU ARE THE TOURNIQUET

How often do we see major movements for change started by women who were hurt by something or someone and who turned their personal loss into a campaign to bring gain to others? Many times we have seen women sitting before Congress testifying with great emotion to some horrific act or unfortunate occurrence that they have experienced, and it has turned them from victims into voices of change where they champion the rights of others who should be spared the pain that they have come to know. Devastation has a way of making you either dispassionate or driven. It can either conquer you and leave you impotent to those around you or cajole you into becoming a powerful vessel for change. Empathy has a force behind it that sympathy can never know. And those of us who have known the depths of loss and suffering must turn this pain into a positive pressure to ensure the betterment of someone else. For we really are the tourniquets for that which makes our own hearts bleed. Within us lies the power and ability to cure what makes us cry.

We have dozens of examples of women doing just that throughout the country. After losing two sons to violent deaths, Clementine Barfield of Detroit founded SOSAD (Save Our Sons and Daughters) in 1987. It has served hundreds of families through the grieving process with counseling and support groups. In 1980, after the death of her thirteen-year-old daughter because of a drunken driver, Candy Lightner led a group of women to found MADD (Mothers Against Drunk

Driving) in California. MADD now has chapters in various states throughout the country and has forced national attention to the devastation and loss that results from drinking and driving. These are only two of many women who have known loss and pain, but have led major crusades for positive change to ensure that others do not have to know the same.

A Pleasure to Serve Through Pain

In 1999 the Reverend Wilma Robena Johnson made history in becoming the first female senior pastor of New Prospect Baptist Church in Detroit. It is still not a common occurrence within the traditional Baptist denomination to ordain women as ministers and even less acceptable that they pastor churches. But she has known phenomenal success; her church has grown in leaps and bounds despite any forces that may have been against her. In watching Pastor J., as she is affectionately called, one can see that her appeal is more than her preaching, which is dynamic and full of passion. For it is after the sermon where you see the strength of her leadership as it is exhibited in acts of humility. Each new member or candidate for baptism is greeted with a full embrace. She does more than hug them, however; she holds them, and it symbolizes the shepherd's care in her for her sheep. Then she steps back and bows as a servant to its master and says, "It is my pleasure to serve as your pastor." In these acts one sees the deep compassion and care that she carries for those she serves.

But there is a story behind this display that makes her leadership style all the more compelling. As a young woman she suffered date rape at the hands of a preacher. Her first introduction to liquor was by a preacher. The very image that would be the most harmful to her as a young adult, she would embody as she accepted her calling so that she could heal. She said that she could have hated preachers, but instead God made her one of them to help heal the hurt of those who might go through the same. Today she is a tourniquet for that which made her own heart bleed.

Compassionate Leadership Breeds Influence

Noted author and leader John C. Maxwell says, "Leadership is influence—nothing more, nothing less."[2] I maintain that it is through compassionate leadership that influence is established. Your ability to motivate people to do something for others will establish you as a leader and a person of influence. And it may just be in the end that your ability to lead will be measured by your ability to influence. However eloquent you may be, however organized, dedicated and knowledgeable, it will be what you care about most that will move people. It will either move them toward you or away from you. It has been said that people don't care how much you know until they know how much you care.

You may impress people with your knowledge, but typically they will not be influenced by it. I saw this clearly some two years ago when I was told that a former student was looking for me. When he finally contacted me through e-mail, it was to tell me that he had married and had children but that one of them, his son, Kyle, had been diagnosed with craniosynostosis and would require having his skull reconstructed. Blake was very concerned and wanted me and others to pray for his son.

I knew that his child would be at Children's Hospital in Detroit and was well aware of their stellar reputation for the treatment of children. I also knew of the brilliance of Dr. Alexa Canady, the neurosurgeon who would perform the surgery. At thirty, Canady became the first African American neurosurgeon in the United States. Though now retired, she had been chief of pediatric neurosurgery for the Children's Hospital of Michigan from 1982 until 1993 when she became chief of neurosurgery until her retirement in 2001. Her success was well chronicled in the medical community. She was considered a visionary in her treatment of brain injuries, and the majority of her patients were ten years old or younger.[3] *Child* magazine selected her as one of the ten best physicians for children, listing her as a specialist in "brain breakthroughs."[4] I told Blake as much as I could about Canady in hopes of putting him at ease about the treatment that his eighteen-month-old son would receive in her care, and I assured him that she was the most qualified doctor in the state and among the best in the world. But it wasn't the knowledge of Canady's skill that mattered most and that assuaged his fears. Rather it was the compassionate manner in which she handled their child and them in the days and hours that preceded Kyle's surgery. Blake said he and his wife, Tracie, "went into her office in complete despair and she very calmly and effectively explained what happened to their son and then assured them how she could fix the problem." The compassionate care of Canady is commonly testified to by her patients. Recent pictures forwarded to me via e-mail show Kyle as a healthy four-year-old boy who now plays hockey and enjoys being big brother to his one-year-old sister, Kaitlyn. Blake and Tracie credit the skill and compassionate leadership of Dr. Alexa Canady, whom they refer to as simply "awesome."

COMPETITION VERSUS COMPASSION

In a small southern Ohio city, two football coaches decided to put human kindness above competition and, in doing so, reminded the athletes, parents and fans that there really is something more important than playing and winning a game. Jake Porter was a senior player on the Northwest High School team who had fragile X syndrome, which is the most common cause of inherited mental retardation. Porter was a faithful member of the football team, attending every practice and dressing in full gear. However, he had never been allowed to take an official snap in a football game and his coach, Dave Frantz, wanted that to change before the end of his final year. Frantz called Derek DeWitt, coach of the Waverly Tigers, and discussed a strategy to allow Porter to get into the end of the game, touch the ball, "take a knee" and end the play. They both knew that Porter could not be hit or put at risk, and thus the call to "take a knee," which requires that play is ended and no contact can be made. But with Waverly leading 49-0, DeWitt was willing to do even more. He met with his competitor at midfield and said, "We'll let him score."[5] Porter entered the game at tailback, received the ball and all twenty players from both teams parted the way to allow this young man to run from the forty-nine-yard line to the end zone to score a touchdown.

DeWitt and his players could have gone for the record shut-out and would have done so, even if he had kept to the original plan to allow Porter to enter the game and "take a knee." But instead of going for a record that would have lasted but a short time, he chose instead a greater act of kindness and compassion that would impact a child for a lifetime.

Both teams were present when a video of these events was shown at Ford Field in Detroit during halftime of 2002 Motor City Bowl football game. Afterward, as we in the stands stood, many with tears in our eyes, Porter led both of the teams in a trot around the stadium. We applauded their every step and the demonstration of compassionate leadership that was shown by the coaches.

A PLATFORM FOR INFLUENCE

Oprah Winfrey is consistently hailed as one of the most powerful and influential women in America by *Fortune* magazine. Each year she is ranked by her monetary value and listed among the richest people in the world. In 2002 she was considered to be the tenth most powerful woman in business in America. In the previous year she was listed as number three. By *Fortune's* terms, which are strictly monetary, her influence has waned, but they would admit that it was purely by her own choice.

Deeply affected by the tragic events of September 11, Oprah reevaluated everything about her life and determined to do things differently. And by differently, one would assume from the parameters through which *Fortune* measures influence, it meant to place other things above profits. She decided to stop doing some things that were very profitable and chose instead to do others. By that decision *Fortune* concluded that she was not losing her power but giving it away.[6]

Despite the magazine's concern for her decision, Oprah Winfrey is in a powerful position financially, having been among the first black female billionaires. But what *Fortune, Forbes, Black Enterprise* and all other magazines that solely base a person's value in terms of finance can never measure is her true influence in the world. It is an influence measured by the depth of her heart and soul, not of her pockets. For the draw to Oprah is not her being the greatest talk show hostess in the history of television. It is her honesty, compassion and empathy for her audiences. She really does love people. Her influence may be measured by the millions of dollars she easily generates through announcing a book to be read through her book club. But her most memorable influence is noted by the thousands of people whom she helps in charitable work each day. She proudly uses her television show to move millions to respond to the needs of others on a regular basis. "It is the most incredible platform for influence that you could imagine," Oprah said, "and it's something that I hold in great esteem and take full responsibility for."[7] Her greatest influence and impact on society can never be measured in dollars and cents, but in what really makes sense: that you can move the world to change if you care enough about what needs changing.

THE RIGHT TO BE HEARD

Pam Farrel defines influence as "earning the right to be heard so that others are moved toward their best."[8] Women earn the right to be heard by the manner in which we have had to earn everything else that we have received or accomplished in life. And African American women have had to earn what our other sisters have been granted by birth. Have we earned the right to be heard in the pulpit? I would say so. For we have carried the weight of churches financially for decades. It has been through our faithful, prayerful support that programs have gone forth and buildings have gone up. We have bought the chickens, cleaned them, cooked them and sold them so that the needs of the church or the desires of the pastor could be met. Have we earned the right to be heard in government? I would say so. We have marched in the streets and stood valiantly against oppression. Those fire hoses that sprayed us and those dogs set on us were never marked "for men only." We too bear the scars of the struggle for freedom in this nation. And we have given our sons and daughters to wars that we did not support but could not stop. Have we earned the right to be heard in the halls of justice? I would say so. We have suffered through the insensitive handling of cases where we have been victimized, raped and molested, only to be made the villains on witness stands time and time again. We have been beaten, shot and murdered and seen the perpetrators treated lightly because the violence was considered domestic and interpreted as our being equally at fault. In every aspect of our lives and in all that affects us, we have

earned the right of influence. It has come through sacrifice and struggle, and we must use it to bring others to their best.

Through the compassion that we have learned through suffering,
through the empathy that we know from the heartache of loss, we
must make a better way for others. We must use the platforms that
we have to influence our churches, schools, cities and national government. These platforms come not just with position but also with
passion and are built through advocacy and a commitment to caring
about our families, communities and country. The greatest of these
platforms are headed not by women with professional titles but by
wives and mothers who are ready and prone to fight for the safety
and security of their children and family. As African American
women we must develop and use our platforms for positive and
sometimes radical change. We must do this because our daughters
are depending on us. We must do this for those whose screams cannot be heard and whose faces cannot be seen. We must lead with
compassion because it is the right thing to do; it is the godly thing to
do. We must do it . . . *because we can!*

QUESTIONS FOR REFLECTION AND DISCUSSION

1. How often are you influenced by the compassion of your leader?
   Can you say that you influence others through examples of compassion?
2. Through your living and giving, have you earned the right to be
   heard? If so, how?
3. In what ways can you can be a tourniquet for that which has made
   your own heart bleed?

8 GROWING IN CONVICTION

Stand up, black woman, for this time demands
The wisdom that speaks from the toil of your hands.

$\mathcal{T}$he tragic death of Senator Paul Wellstone from Minnesota saddened the entire nation and brought to mind the missing ingredient in the lives of most of our present-day leaders: conviction. Over and over the eulogies about this man spoke of the single thing that separated him from so many others: he was a man of conviction. Upon hearing that, so many other things might run through your mind, for you know that with the tag of *conviction* come those things that are understood and misunderstood about you. Your mind conjures pictures of the prophets of old who dared stand alone in the midst of the crowd as a single voice of God's warning to his people. For a distinguishing factor in those who live a life of conviction is solitude, and often that is not by choice. Admired perhaps by many, those with conviction are often followed by few.

Conviction is different from commitment because it carries you further than what commitment may demand. One's commitment to something is sometimes contingent on the parameters established by another. But conviction results from core beliefs that are singular and personal, that remain despite what others say, do or prefer. Conviction is what calls for you to stand alone and against public polls and popularity to defend what your conscience calls you to say and do. It is conviction that feeds and fuels your courage, and it cannot be contained by the constraints that may be set by another.

Conviction is rooted in faith. It is action compelled by faith—our faith in who we are and whose we are. It is the answer to what we believe that God has seeded in us to do. It is that thing which has taken its deepest root in us and serves as a gyroscope toward persistent action, that thing which becomes our choice when we have other options. That's why it is imperative for us to believe that God has chosen us to do special things in this world. We absolutely must see ourselves as he sees us and not as history and tradition dictate. The very best leadership that we can know is tied to conviction.

> LEADERSHIP IS TIED TO CONVICTION.
>
> **Delorese Ambrose,** Ed.D.,
> *Leadership: The Journey Inward*

LIVE TO LEAD

If you have felt during your life that you are on Earth simply to follow the path of least resistance, then change that thinking today. If you have been taught that you must go along to get along, decide that you like your own company and commit to doing things differently. Isolation often provides time for clarity of thought without other voices opining about what is good or relevant. There are things that you see every day that you know you can change, or at the very least impact positively, but you leave it to that imaginary person called somebody and deny yourself the opportunity to make your mark. It's time that you live differently and that you live to lead. People with conviction don't often have a choice, for many times they march by a different drumbeat that pulls them away from the band. Change takes place one minute, one moment and one person at a time. If you decide to live to lead, you will be driven to make the change or be the change that the world needs.

I once heard someone say that the richest place in the world is the cemetery because of all of the unused potential, talents and gifts that are buried there. Many of the leaders we need are buried there, but worse yet, some are not buried but are dead on their feet because they have failed to use the gifts that they have to lead. They have remained unconvinced that they are the ones for the job. Don't die until you lead!

LEARN TO LEAD

In earlier chapters we have discussed how God has given us everything we need to be great leaders in our communities, schools, churches and country. But having what we need and not using it does us no good. Sometimes what we have needs to be revealed to us and then it needs to be developed to the point of its greater use. I am reminded of the call to Moses to lead the children of Israel from bondage to promise. He had literally run from himself and was on the back side of the desert when God called him. Afraid of what God was asking him to do, he began to question if he was the right one for the job. The first thing he questioned was his own identity and purpose, asking, "Who am I that I should go unto Pharaoh, and that I should bring forth the children of Israel out of Egypt?" (Exodus 3:11). Moses then asked what he would say, and he continued to offer God reasons why he was not the one for the job. But then God showed Moses how he had been carrying his tool of leadership all along when he asked what was in Moses' hand (see Exodus 4:2). The thing that would be used to immediately distinguish him as being God's leader was the rod that he carried and used for lesser purposes. God had already equipped him for great and mighty things, but Moses' thinking about himself and what he possessed did not match God's purpose for it and him. But after Moses fully received what his intended purpose was and understood that he had been enabled by God to lead, he then did so with power and conviction.

In a like manner, we are equipped by God to lead, but what we have come to accept with comfort about ourselves and our skills is not a match for what God has intended. He has considered us higher than we perceive ourselves. For him to use us to do great and mighty things, we must cultivate what we already have and develop ourselves into the leaders that we need to be. We must learn to use our "rods" effectively. We must seek the wisdom of God about what he desires us to do and what he has equipped us with, and then move to use our skills, intellect, talents and gifts to the greater use.

I was seated next to Phyllis Schlafly at a luncheon and asked her about her opinions on leadership. She said whereas "some people say there are born leaders, I was not one of them. I had to learn to lead." She was at one time very shy and did not consider herself to be a leader. Many others have this testimony. A deeply rooted belief took hold of them and rose in response to a need, a crisis or a situation that tested them, and it catapulted them into an action so bold that others took note of it. This conviction goaded them into finding ways to make a difference or to bring about a change. Even for those of us who are considered "born leaders," it is important for us to study leadership and other leaders—those examples set before us in books and in life that can enrich us as we develop ourselves into outstanding leaders.

LOVE TO LEAD

There are few people who would say they love to lead. Those who say they do are often referring to their love of being out front and their passion for being seen. Because leadership carries such a heavy and awesome weight, and because the responsibilities are often so staggering, few would say they love the chore of leadership. To suggest that one loves to lead reminds me of the Scripture that says we should count it a joy to have trials and tribulations (see James 1:2). The joy comes from the outcome of the trials and not the trials themselves. To love to lead is to realize the result of the effort of your work and to see the impact of your hand on someone or something and to know its value.

Leadership is not at all about some ego trip for those who like to see their names in lights. For real leaders are driven by outcome and understand that it's not about lights upon them, but the Light in them that brings others to see things and themselves better. The best leaders close their eyes to the glamour of being known, while at the same time they have the wisdom to use their notoriety for the betterment of others. To suggest that you love to lead is to speak to the passion that connects your conviction to the cause. Laurie Beth Jones said, "A leader who is not passionately committed to the cause will not draw much commitment from others."[1]

THE PATHS OF PASSION

Fervor and *passion* are the words most used to describe or define conviction. Today *fervor* is most used to describe the frivolous fan of sport or the misguided religious zealot. The passion that drives one to serve the downtrodden, to stand for the weak, to speak for the silent is not seen as much or as often as it once was. The paths of passion and conviction are not cluttered and are truly the roads less traveled. But we have had examples of those who walked this path and whose footsteps beckon our emulation.

Mother Teresa chose her path of passion through work with the poor and helpless in the forgotten valleys of Calcutta. Whereas it was natural for nuns to take a vow of poverty and service, her conviction to aid the poor was far from natural. It was a walk from which she never strayed. She never took a break, never sought relief because of burnout. In 1979 when she was awarded the Nobel Peace Prize, she reminded the world about those who littered the path on which she walked: "I choose the poverty of our poor people. But I am grateful to receive [the Nobel] in the name of the hungry, the naked, the homeless, of the crippled, of the blind, of the lepers, of all those people who feel unwanted, unloved, uncared-for throughout society, people that have become a burden to the society and are shunned by everyone."[2]

Paul Robeson was both celebrated and condemned for his walk of passion, when in the 1930s and 1940s he was perhaps the best-known and most widely respected black American. However, there were times in which he was vilified for his frank views on issues, which ran contrary to public opinion. As a brilliant scholar, athlete, actor, musician and civil rights activist, Robeson attacked the vicious and racist practices of his country with fervor, in spite of the fact that he and his family were spared most of the venom and brutality that others were experiencing. Led by his passion and conviction, Robeson stood on principles and politics that were not embraced by most in this country, and it led him toward communism, which he felt more closely aligned him with fairness and justice to all people. Regardless of his communist leanings, which led to his being charged during the infamous McCarthy hearings, he refused to leave America because it was where his father was born a slave and his people had sacrificed their lives to build it to the great country it had become. He would stay and fight in this country for the freedom and justice for all people, though he was blacklisted and banned from participation in most things that would have allowed him a good living. In the end, his conviction and passion and all that he did to break down the barriers of racism were

diminished by his radical politics, and he was at last dismissed and
pronounced both "an American triumph and tragedy."[3]

Though few remember her name, Viola Liuzzo became a martyr of
the civil rights movement and the only white female murdered during that struggle for freedom and justice. A wife and mother of five
children, Liuzzo watch televised scenes of brutal beatings and attacks
upon blacks in Selma, Alabama, as they were trying to register to
vote. She decided that she would leave her home in Detroit to drive
to Alabama to assist in the voter registration in Selma. Painted by the
FBI as a mentally unstable woman, she was considered as just the
kind of northern rabble-rouser Southern whites and the Klansmen
loved to hate. Aware of the danger of her personal involvement in
Selma, Liuzzo chose to drive blacks from Selma to Montgomery and
back during their campaign for registration. That stretch of land became her path of passion and death when she was shot by a Klans-
man from a passing vehicle.

A couple of years ago, after I had been commissioned to write a
song in her honor and memory, I was able to speak with her son, Anthony, who moved me by saying that what bothered him most was
that nobody seems to remember her name. It is unfortunate that the
names and faces of the passionate few are often not remembered. It
is common that they are looked upon as mentally unfit, and portraits
are painted of them as being less desirable for the better and higher
places of society. But when that paint dries, it peels, and the truth is
always uncovered. Viola Liuzzo and many other women, whose
names we do not know but whose untiring devotion to freedom we
applaud, walked tall and shone brightly during one of the darkest
times of our country's history.

Tried for treason, sabotage and violent conspiracy, Nelson Mandela was found guilty and given a life sentence in prison because of

his fight against apartheid in South Africa. However, during his imprisonment, his conviction never waned. His appeal to those who knew even the limited freedom of black South Africans grew, and his fight crossed international borders into other countries that began to demand his release. For almost thirty years Mandela endured the penalty of maximum-security lockup, but the fight in him could not be contained behind prison walls, and he covertly kept his battle going. In February 1990, I stood before my television watching him and his wife, Winnie, walk from the prison in the midst of thousands who cheered on both sides of the road. His path of passion would be chronicled in his autobiography *Long Walk to Freedom* and told by authors and journalists throughout the world. After decades of being treated as a criminal and held in the most secure prisons, Mandela became president of the country that had held him prisoner. His walk to freedom on that February day was strong and steady. Even after many years of imprisonment, he had a dignity and grace that could not be denied.

What of this path of passion and where does it lead? Although it is not a crowded path, I surmise that many travel this road whose names we will never know, because those so committed to a dream or a cause do so without the fanfare and acknowledgement of others. What we see in Mandela is that a convicted spirit cannot be contained by prison. Mother Teresa taught us that the passion to serve can withstand poverty, sickness and hopelessness. The lives of Paul Robeson and Viola Liuzzo demonstrate that banishment and the threat of death will not thwart a love for freedom and the drive to see justice for all.

A LEGACY TO LEAD

For women to continue to make the gains that we need to make and to reach the planes and levels that we desire and deserve, it is imperative that we not settle for the few spaces that are typically "allowed" or granted. We can never be satisfied with seeing just *one* of us climb to a higher plateau when there should be *many* of us there. It is always fitting and proper to celebrate the new paths that are made by pioneers. We applaud those who pierce the glass ceilings, but it is no longer enough for us to rejoice at the splintered glass that falls beneath to the rest of us. We need to also come through the ceiling. Far too often we have seen one woman become the first to do something, and then decades will pass before the second woman does the same. And in too many cases, there is never anyone else who follows.

Therefore, as we reach new stages of accomplishments, it is imperative that we make concentrated efforts to broaden the opening for other women. Mentoring is a must! Belle Rose Ragins, a professor of management at the University of Wisconsin-Milwaukee, says, "Everyone who makes it has a mentor and for women and minorities, mentoring is nearly mandatory. For women and minorities face barriers to advancement that can be overcome with the help of a mentor."[4]

PASS THE BALL ALONG

Crabs in a barrel or bucket are known to claw at one another and keep each other from climbing up and out of the bucket. It is sad to note that in many cases we have a crab-barrel mentality about one another; we will attempt to pull others down as we see them approaching the top. Instead we must use our shoulders as ladders to assist the ascension and not impede it.

During the introductions of each star at the Women's National Basketball Association (WNBA) first All-Star game, each player would take a ball to the center of the court and place it in the hands of a young girl. The advent of the WNBA was a long time coming. There were countless women who had enjoyed great college athletic careers and who, after graduating, had no option but to leave America to pursue a professional basketball career in another country. The success of the league will be in the financial support of those who love the game, but it will also be ensured through legacy, just as it is in other sports. There must be a historical beginning for everything, but there also needs to be a passing of the ball so that future generations will have and enjoy the same.

> IT IS ONLY WHEN WE DEVELOP OTHERS THAT WE PERMANENTLY SUCCEED.
>
> **Harvey Firestone**

A leader of conviction doesn't want to die until she leads, but she also doesn't want to see what she leads die. Some mistakenly believe that their leadership skills are proven when things fall apart in their absence. That is far from truth. To the misguided few, it may measure their importance to an organization or body. But if anything, it demonstrates that too much is centered in and dependent on a single person. The focus is the (wo)man and not the plan.

In 1984 I founded a semiprofessional ensemble that traveled, made several recordings, did TV appearances and was considered by many to be an outstanding group. I was the songwriter, arranger and director, the motivational leader and organizer of most of everything we did. Unfortunately I was burned out after almost five years. To the disappointment of the other members, I informed them that I could not go on. I suggested that they continue, but they did not. A group of that magnitude and that level of excellence should not have died at my departure, and I have always looked at its doing so as a flaw in my leadership. Although I asked that they continue, I never prepared them to do so.

Develop a Plan to Mentor

Our plans for leadership must include more than ourselves. Regardless of how inspired, intelligent and committed a single person may be to something, there should always be a preparation of another to participate in the program if it is to be maintained or to grow and prosper. Moses was an integral part of God's plan to free the Israelites from Egypt and to lead them to their land of promise. But he was not the one who would ultimately walk them into that land. He had to prepare Joshua. Women tend to understand the importance of mentoring, but we simply do not consider the importance of our helping and mentoring one another. We will mentor a man far quicker than we will another woman. We have no problem preparing Joshua, but we need to also prepare Jessica, and we need to plan to do so.

Having a plan to mentor means that we will sacrifice the time and be proactive in seeking out those people with potential for leadership and in offering assistance in their development. It means putting them on a regimented plan for achievement, holding them accountable for what they do, correcting their errors and applauding their success and accomplishment. A mentoring plan needs to include our knowledge of the strengths and weakness of our protégé, and we need to be able to honestly assess her so that we can help her maximize one and minimize the other. I believe in actually doing this in writing. I have taken the Scripture in Habakkuk about "writing down the revelation" to heart, because it is only in writing things down that good ideas become good plans (2:2 NIV). And a good plan is much easier to follow than an idea. But the written plan cannot and should not take the place of one-on-one sharing and shadowing, where time is spent talking things through and role modeling. For an important part of the mentoring plan should include the accessibility of the mentor to the protégé.

Raising Up Other Leaders

In overwhelming numbers, women are still being mentored by men. Often this is because men occupy most of the powerful positions of leadership and authority. In some instances, women do not choose to bother themselves with assisting other women and often exhibit the same traits and practices of sexism as men do. It is discouraging and disappointing to see this among women, and black women in particular. After struggling to accomplish a feat or to secure a position, it is nothing short of disgusting to then turn our backs on other women who need us as role models and mentors to pave their road to accomplish the same. It is small-minded and shortsighted when we do not consciously open the door for others like us, and it limits our legacy and destroys the hopes and dreams of young women who will follow us.

I had a conversation with a female pastor about the fact that she did not have any women visible in leadership at her church. It was run just like most other black churches in that it was predominately female, but was led by men, with a single exception. Her response was that she wanted a female to be "all that" before she placed her in a leadership position. But I pointed out that her men were not "all that," yet she chose to use them. She had unconsciously set a higher standard for the women of her church than she had for the men. Without her help, the women would never meet the standard they needed to satisfy. Prior to our discussion, she did not have a conscious need to mentor women in leadership; she had failed to realize that she was actually mentoring the men.

We see this not only in churches but also in other organizations that women or African Americans lead. We tend to extend ourselves beyond what is necessary to demonstrate the fact that we are "fair," so we are more inclusive of others who are not like us or those who

124

resemble us. White males don't have a problem surrounding themselves with other white men, especially when they think they are
qualified for the job. But women and minorities who are blended into
their environment will rarely do the same. If we ever become convicted about our roles as leaders, we will ensure that there is a suc-
cession of those like us to follow us in a legacy of leadership.

WE MUST SHARE WHAT WE HAVE

I have found few willing examples of mentors, in part because it is
not a role for the average person to take. Talent and smarts do not a
mentor make. Mentoring involves self-sacrifice and altruism. It is
best done by men and women who perceive who they are and are
comfortable with what they see. They then desire to see the same
thing in someone else.

I am reminded of Martha Jean Steinberg, a radio personality turned
preacher, pastor and teacher to thousands for over four decades until
her death in 2000. "The Queen" was at first her radio handle, but it
became not simply what many *called* her but who she *was* to many.
She loved herself and had no problem saying it. She appreciated first
of all the struggles of her life and what she was able to accomplish in
spite of them, and she told everyone else that they could do the same.
Six feet tall, elegant and truly regal, yet down to earth at the same
time, the Queen was able to reach the masses like few others could.
Though most of her listeners were the blue-collar, common, everyday
folk, she wanted everyone to have what she had: self-esteem, power,
influence and money. And daily she told us to believe in what was best
about ourselves so we could become what we believed.

More than preaching to others, the Queen mentored many. Often
you would hear people speak of how she gave them their start in the
radio business. After she purchased her own station in 1997—and

was clearly a giant in Detroit and in her arena nationally—she still took time to personally encourage women, in particular, to follow her steps and their hearts. I had a friend who was a radio personality in North Carolina who came to Detroit to visit and asked me to see if she could meet with the Queen. I was startled at the request and didn't expect the Queen to acknowledge my call, much less accept it. But she invited the young lady to come in and, to my surprise and her delight, talked with her at length about the unlimited possibilities that lay before her. The Queen was passionate about the treatment of women and this passion goaded her not only to talk about it, but also to help other women change their thoughts about who they were and what they were able to accomplish. And the Queen could do this because she desired to see herself reflected in someone else.

Kenya Jordana James sees her own unlimited potential and at age thirteen has already decided that it is her responsibility to help others see theirs. Two years ago, she was dissatisfied with magazines she felt did not adequately speak to her interests, so she founded *Blackgirl* magazine to address historical, cultural and entertainment issues for teens. It is also her goal to start her own clothing line. She has an enormous vision about her life and what she can accomplish. But the most interesting thing about Kenya is that, at her tender age, she feels a need and senses a responsibility to help others. She says that she wants to be "the best role model for teens and younger children so that they can become the next kings, queens or presidents."[5]

A LADDER FOR OTHERS

In October 2002, dozens of African American poets gathered in Detroit to celebrate the thirtieth anniversary of Lotus Press, which had served as a vehicle for introducing their works to the public. It had come about as the direct result of the passion of one woman, Naomi

Long Madgett, an English professor who wanted to encourage and
expose the talents of her students over the years. Most knew they
never would have had the opportunity to get published had it not
been for Madgett. However, she deflected any and all of the light cast
upon her by saying, "It gives me joy to be able to introduce new poets
to the public. I'm not intended to be a star. I'm intended to be a ladder for others."[6]

Becoming a mentor and role model means we will choose to be the
ladder and not the star. It means we will allow ourselves to be used
to further a cause or spread a message that is above and beyond ourselves. It means we will not expect other women to break new
ground for themselves but will allow them to enjoy the light from the
glass ceiling that we have, through pain and progress, shattered.

Networking and positive reinforcement of each other can be done
in addition to or as a substitute for mentoring. Although I personally
mentor several men and women, I have built a reinforcement net-
work through my Breakfast And A Word gatherings by bringing together women of all cultures, classes and religious backgrounds for a
period of encouragement, inspiration and empowerment. Each
month, the focus is on a single word: all of the music, poetry, dance
or drama, as well as the inspirational message, are centered around
that word. The word is typically one of enrichment and encouragement, such as *promise, faith, courage* and *purpose*. I don't allow any
negativity on any subject matter, and even those that relate to our
health are projected positively. For two hours, doctors, lawyers,
teachers, politicians, mothers, grandmothers, ministers, nurses,
postal workers and others come together to focus on what we have
in common as women, and we lift it above our differences. We are
strengthened by each other's presence and made to see only the best
that we are and can become.

CONVICTED TO A CAUSE

After one such breakfast I was particularly moved by a phone call from Alberta Griffee, a ninety-year-old woman who had come to her first breakfast. She was calling to purchase tickets for herself and others for the next month's event. "Sylvia, I just want to tell you how much I enjoyed the breakfast and how thankful I am that you are doing this, because we need it." Immediately I was struck by her use of the word *we:* what could she need at age ninety that I or the others could give her? I then realized that the lesson for me in her call was about perspective and conviction. She was committed to the cause of women being empowered and made to feel good about who and what we are. This obviously was not a new belief or an enlightenment she received at age ninety, and it wasn't something that she was going to leave behind at that age either. From her perspective, *we* are tied together in and through a common cause. She had come to know that what benefited one of us was to the benefit of all of us.

Dr. Dorothy Height is a model of being convicted to a cause. At age ninety-one she is the chairperson and president emerita of the National Council of Negro Women, an organization to which she has been devoted for over sixty years. She is slowed only by movement due to her age; her voice, spirit, wisdom and drive are unabated. Dr. Height, along with Alberta Griffee, sees the struggle as being about *us.* Her belief in the cause of civil rights and advancement for women began when she was a young girl. Mary McCloud Bethune, first president of the Council, *put her hand on her,* and Dr. Height was drawn into a powerful circle of passion and advocacy. She has remained committed to that cause to this day.

Jane Stone, director of resource development at the United Way of Ocean County, New Jersey, said, "We all need role models who can guide us in that journey of both personal and professional development. It doesn't happen by accident. For too many people, it doesn't happen at all."[7] It is imperative that, through role modeling and mentoring, we lessen the struggle of those who would follow in our steps. We will do this if we are so convicted to the cause, to seeing ourselves in others and to being the ladder for someone else to climb. We will do this whenever we can . . . because we can.

QUESTIONS FOR REFLECTION AND DISCUSSION

1. To what is your conviction tied and in what is it rooted?
2. Are you among the walking dead, or have you decided to live to lead? What will your next step be?
3. Reflect on the tools God has given you for leadership that you have been using for lesser purposes. What is your "rod"?
4. Do you love to lead? If so, what does that mean to you?
5. What are you passionate about today?
6. In what ways are you making a concentrated effort to "pass your ball along"?
7. How are you making mentoring a part of your leadership plan?
8. Is there something about you and your life that you believe is worthy of emulation? If so, what are you doing to raise up other leaders?

9   OVERCOMING CHALLENGES

You have the drive and you have the plan
Stand up, black woman . . . because you can!

I admit to being a fan of Simon Peter, and I have enjoyed hearing the many and varied sermons preached on his impetuosity, his strengths and his weaknesses. The black preacher, in particular, has been quite creative in teaching and preaching many lessons on the actions and sayings of Peter. You can ask two or three theologians to look at the same text involving Peter and they will each look differently at what he did or said. But there is one thing that I believe they will all agree on: Peter was a leader. He wasn't one because he belonged to a group of leaders but because he stood out from the others. For good or bad, Peter distinguished himself because he took risks. Real leaders are risk takers in their thinking first and then their actions. They believe there is something beyond the box of tradition and customs, and they dare to think and move outside that box.

Perhaps one of the greater challenges of leadership is taking risk. Is there anything more common to African American women than the fact that we take risks? Doing so seems to be a part of our daily regimen. We raise children without husbands and insurance. We take risks. We often, by necessity, attempt to do things that require more with less. We take risks. Some of the risks we take are not in our best interests, but we can be so determined to accomplish something that we will perform a task in ways that others would deem unimaginable and impossible. At the same time we can be so loyal to a system and way of working that we hinder our growth and productivity. And in many ways that too is a risk.

This entire book has been a challenge to us to stand and lead. Neither of those things would present a test for us beyond what we already find familiar. Any honest recording of our history and practices will find us standing. It will also reveal us to be leaders, though mostly covertly, in an attempt to secure the men in our lives or to secure our lives through supporting men. We've led without titles and we've led through those who had titles. In churches, we led from the pews, figuratively and literally, for there were situations in which our men could not read and we would call out the words to them from our seats. They could lead even when they could not read. But because we were women, we were not even allowed to stand up and speak in the worship service of some churches because doing so would "usurp authority" over the man. And because we love our men and want to see them in positions of authority, we accepted this designated place.

> THE CALL TO STAND IS NOTHING NEW AND IT SHOULD NOT SOUND SO FOREIGN TO YOU.

The lack of women in leadership has not been wiped away in the passing of time. Some of our largest denominations still practice sexism in this twenty-first century. They do so to the point of their preferring a weak leader, or in some cases no leader at all, to a woman being placed above a man. There are churches being led "by committee"—a group of men—because of their inability to find the "right man" for the job. Search committees have worked for years trying to find the best man, when in some cases there simply were no men to find. However, they would not allow themselves to consider that the best man for the job was actually a woman.

One can understand the reluctance of men to accept women in certain places, when it comes from their assertion that God would not have women in leadership positions in ministry. They are holding on to deeply rooted beliefs about what God would want in his church. But this becomes a moot point when one sees that the differences in treatment of men and women are not only in choices of leadership. In October 2002 I was the mistress of ceremonies for a benefit concert at a church in Ohio. As I always do, I asked where the proper place would be for me to stand and was told that I should not approach the podium, which was situated in the pulpit and reserved for the pastor of the church. They eventually found me a small stand to use, and that was sufficient for me.

This was not an unusual move because many churches do not allow women to speak from the podium where their pastors or other men do. It has even been a long-held tradition in some churches not to allow a woman to walk into the pulpit at all. But something happened during the service that made their actions and practices offensive. While I was waiting for the small stand to be brought up before the program began, I sat down in a chair at the very end of the pulpit. The pastor came and told me that they did not allow women to sit in their pulpit and that I had to move immediately. I stood up and apologized to him and found a seat at the end of a pew behind the choir. At least twice during the concert, one of the officials of the church, a man who was able to freely move in and out of the pulpit, took cigarette breaks and smoked in an area of the church directly behind the pulpit. Because his smoke was so strong and bothersome to the choir, I would have to get up and close the door so that it would not choke the singers. It was clear that the practices of that church, as they related to women, were rooted not in a misguided interpretation of Scripture but in a misogynistic idea of authority.

The mere presence of a woman sitting in a pulpit was condemned, but a man could smoke within feet of the pulpit during the worship service and it was condoned.

This is a conspicuous demonstration of the sexism that has been tolerated for too long—and it must be challenged. It must be challenged because we need our churches to remain strong and vital to our communities. We are losing people in great numbers who are completely turned off by how things are being done; they are choosing to stay at home. These are not individuals who are new to the worship experience, but are seasoned Christians who have been raised in the church environment and who can no longer tolerate or condone its present practices.

In fairness it must be stated that the bigotry displayed toward women in churches is just a fraction of what has caused many to turn away. There are many among those who have departed because of discontent who are capable of leading in a way that could make the needed significant changes to the church, and many of them are women. They are young women who have seen their mothers, aunts and grandmothers sacrifice for decades to sustain a church, only to be discarded as quickly as a vote is taken in a business meeting. They no longer believe, as did their older relatives, that the decisions and choices of the male leadership are solely grounded in Scripture, and they reject it. But in rejecting those teachings and through their departure they are abandoning an important institution that we need to keep strong in the African American community.

Challenge—the act of confronting, or demanding what is just and right—is a part of the very fabric of our country, and the right to do so is intrinsic to who we are as Americans. Our political system is built on challenge, and every vote cast is merely our means of contesting how things are and expressing our hopes of how we desire things to be. The right of protest and challenge is important for us and we must not desert this right, but we also cannot be threatened or put off by challenges to us. In the manner in which our challenges serve to strengthen our government, our churches, our judicial system and our schools, they can make us strong also. So we must challenge the systems that would prevent us from leading. And we must do so with dignity, strength and grace.

BUT WITH SAND DRIFTING AND NO TIME TO WASTE . . .

There is urgency to this challenge, and it is precipitated by both lack and love. There are so many needs in society and within our community that we no longer have the luxury of time to wait for someone other than ourselves to fill those needs. We have longed for our men to be the answer to what afflicts us. And in many ways they have been. But too many of them are missing from our homes, our churches, our families, our lives. Far too many are incarcerated and too few are being educated. We need leadership from more than just our men and we need it now. The diligence with which we have

COME FROM BENEATH THE SWEAT AND GRUNT BLACK WOMAN, IT'S TIME TO STAND OUT FRONT.

served our families has demonstrated our love for them. But the manner in which we have also served our churches, schools and country exemplifies that we love them as well. We can and should be good mothers, but we are capable of also being good pastors, principals, judges, senators and presidents.

We have longed for another Martin Luther King Jr. and have searched for his leadership in and among men who have followed him. It is time for us to consider that in Martin's absence our greatest help will come instead through Marsha, Maegan, Michelle or Martha. I am not suggesting that we push our men aside or that we push them away. I am saying that the time we have spent coaxing and covering them can best be spent working side by side with them to expeditiously move our agenda forward to accomplish more, quicker. The bottom line is that we must accept a greater responsibility for the leadership in our communities. And there are two basic reasons why we should: because we care and because we can.

BECAUSE WE CARE

HIV/AIDS is an epidemic throughout the world, resulting in more than twenty-five million deaths, most of which have occurred in Africa. It is a secret scourge within our United States community as well. Although African Americans represent only 12 percent of the U.S. population, we accounted for half of the new HIV cases reported in the United States in 2001. Almost 38 percent of all AIDS victims in this country are African American. In 2001 almost two thirds (64 percent) of all American women with AIDS were black.[1] And AIDS is the leading cause of death among black women between twenty-five and forty years of age.[2]

Our silence on this subject is inexcusable and unforgivable. We can no longer afford to hide in shame and not discuss the drug abuse and illicit sexual behavior that often leads to our contracting this horrible disease. A theologically grounded program that is culturally appropriate has been developed to generate this discussion. Under the leadership of Monifa A. Jumanne, the Health Education Leadership Program (HELP) at the Interdenominational Theological Center, in cooperation with the U.S. Center for Disease Control and Prevention, developed a comprehensive teaching resource called "Affirming a Future with Hope: HIV and Substance Abuse Prevention for African

American Communities of Faith." I have been afforded the opportunity of being a part of the workshops of this program. It is outstanding because it addresses HIV education and prevention through a curriculum that also blends in Scripture and spiritual principles. Its primary goal is to promote a relationship with God as the "sure foundation" for HIV prevention. Jumanne's work in faith-based HIV prevention has earned commendation from the mayor of Atlanta and the U.S. House of Representatives. It has been established primarily as a vehicle through which the black church will address this epidemic among us. And we will do so . . . because we care.

The illiteracy rate in this country, particularly in urban areas, is staggering. Within cities that are predominately black, it can come close to including half the population. Illiteracy feeds the crime and decadence in and about our neighborhoods and it fills our jails and prisons. There are places in which we can volunteer to teach adults to read and to make a small effort to eradicate illiteracy among us. We will do this if we care.

African Americans make up a disproportionately large part of the prison population in the United States, creating a void within our homes, churches and schools. Our presence on college campuses is a mere shadow of what it should be, especially among our boys and men. We can argue that the justice system functions best for those who have money, and consequently does not work as effectively for men and women of color, but there are things that we can do to stem the tide of the massive influx of our men into prisons. We must reinvent the village that we once had, which served as a tremendous support system for each other. Through it we looked after each other's children and served as a safety net for those appearing to fall through society's cracks. The village has become inoperable because we do not regard one another as we used to. We trusted one another to help discipline our children and to keep a watchful eye out for them. We taught our children to be respectful of all adults, no matter who they were, and they responded to adults with reverence and admiration for their age and wisdom. Because respect is lacking, fewer of us are willing to subject ourselves to the verbal abuse that may come from our "interfering" with a child who is not our own.

"I GOT MINE" VERSUS "YOU ARE MINE"

What made the village so wonderful and powerful was that there was no child who was not our own. We were so linked together in mind, goal and purpose that we acted as a single family. We are splintered today in ways that have manifested and magnified a greed and self-ishness within us, and it is detrimental to all of us. We are not inclu-sive in our thinking of those about us anymore. Too often the attitude displayed is "I got mine so you get yours." And we have even gone so far as to close the doors through which we have walked. They slam in the faces of others who are coming behind us. The "I got mine" mindset says that we can live independently of one another and all will be well. But that is not true. For through that thinking we are be-coming separated by chasms of education and money; resentment then breeds on both sides of these divides. But if we return to the at-mosphere in which "you are mine," then we will go from being inde-pendent to being interdependent, and the village will return to the highly regarded place it once held. We will then realize and respond to the fact that if you are grown and still cannot read, then my books cannot be enjoyable to me. Therefore I must do something to help you read. We will see that our freedom is inextricably tied to one an-other's, and thus we will support a good educational system that will help keep fewer of us from being imprisoned.

Each year hundreds of African Americans will die of leukemia, sickle cell anemia and other blood-related diseases because they need bone marrow transplants. It is estimated that African Americans receive these transplants only 3.3 percent of the time as compared to a rate of 85 to 88 percent for whites.[3] Many of these deaths could be prevented if more of us would register as donors. We are reluctant because of our fears and lack of education as to the process. However, because of past transgressions against us, we also are suspicious of some medical procedures and there is doubt within our community about the fairness of the distribution of organs and tissues that are donated. But what we must come to understand is that, because some characteristics of tissue may vary among ethnic groups, it is more likely that a person will find a match among those of his or her own race. Therefore in these cases nobody can help us but us, and we need to arise to meet this need among us. We need to register in the National Marrow Donor Program before one of our children, relatives or friends becomes deathly ill and is looking for a match to save his or her life.

In 2000 I saw a young lady in a grocery store who I had once worshiped with, and she was using the motorized scooter that the store provides for those with walking difficulties. I asked her if she had sprung her foot or something, and she looked at me in surprise and said, "Haven't you heard that I have bone cancer? If I don't get a marrow transplant, I will die." I was shocked, not only because I had not heard about it but also because she was so calm in telling me. She said that a church was going to hold a drive to sign people up to see if there could be a match. I told her I was already in the registry and that I wished I would have been a match for her so that I could make that donation. Unfortunately, even before the church could hold the marrow drive, she took a turn for the worse and died. She and others might have been spared had the African American community stepped up to the plate to register—a simple procedure that sustains life. We should do this because, larger than the fear that may loom within us, a heart beats for each other; more than we fear, we care.

Because We Can

Many years ago I was the choral director at a Christian high school. One day a week I required my students to rehearse standing on risers for the entire class period. Although they were young, healthy and energetic, this was not something they enjoyed doing. Yet they submitted themselves to this discipline and were conditioned to the fact that on Fridays it was expected of them. Much to their surprise and dismay, I walked into the classroom on a Wednesday and announced that rehearsal would be on risers. You can imagine the response to this request. With great reluctance they pulled themselves from their chairs and stepped onto the risers. Finally one of the singers asked why they would have to stand on a Wednesday, when the "rule" was that Friday was the day to stand. The class became quiet in anticipation of my response. I surprised them by saying only three words: "Because you can." They expected me to demonstrate my authority by saying, "Because I said so." Instead I empowered them by reinforcing their ability and their discipline. There was no physical reason they could not stand for an hour. They had been sitting all day in their other classes and I, on the other hand, had been standing. I knew they were as healthy as I was and by that hour of the day, even more energetic. I was teaching them that their ability to do anything and all things in life was tied to a decision—one that they needed to make for themselves. They would and could do what was asked of them in life either because of the person asking or because of their own will to do it. They would either submit themselves to the will of others throughout their lives or they would take control of their own.

"Because you can" became our battle cry for the rest of the year. I often heard students yelling it at others in the halls or in other classes. I knew that sometimes it was in mockery of me, but I was pleased at their having understood the message. It is a motto that governs my life and a message I have continued to share over the years. God has empowered us and equipped us to do and be far more than what we have settled for. We have limited ourselves by the choices that others make for us and have not walked into the realm of our highest living because others have determined that we can't, when in actuality we can.

I dedicated this book to Tuesdays because that is the day of the week I set aside as my vision day—the day in which I remind myself of all that I can do. On Tuesdays I tune out the negative influences—whether people, television or radio—and focus only on those things that strengthen my will to become what I believe God has seeded in me. I limit contact with people via phone and e-mail and restrict the possibility of that day and time being marred by those who cannot see in me what I see in myself. It is a day when I feed my dreams through faith statements, Scripture and prayer. It is on this day when I remind myself of the possibilities against all odds: "I can do all things through Christ which strengtheneth me" (Philippians 4:13).

Yet I am by no means a solitary example of what can be done when one is empowered by God to move. The Bible, the church and the world are full of them. But there can and should be more of those who will not fear the giant in their promise, because they will see and bear witness to the giant within themselves.

In the summer of 1992, the Fort Worth school board needed a principal to head Dunbar High School, which had been rife with corruption and illicit behavior among students and staff. Despite protestations against hiring a female, they turned to Shirley Knox-Benton for leadership during the darkest times that school had experienced.

Students were failing and teachers were not motivated to teach. But in the face of low test scores, high truancy and a minimal respect for authority, Knox-Benton stepped up to the challenge of turning that school around by implementing a simple motto: *It can be done!* Through developing strategies that increased school morale and parental involvement, Dunbar raised the school's test scores, its image and the overall student body self-esteem. It is now one of the top-ranked schools in the state of Texas, and Shirley Knox-Benton, who has been honored with dozens of awards and commendations, was the Texas State Administrator of the Year in 2001 and one of ten Readers Digest American Heroes in Education.

AND NOW IT'S TIME FOR YOU TO LEAD

Before we can really conceive what we can become, we must call upon a sight beyond our natural vision. It is imperative that we see beyond our heritage, our education and our upbringing to the impossible that is gestating within us. We have been prepared for leadership all of our lives through struggle and sacrifice. We have waited patiently and stood behind and in support of others. And now is the time for *us* to lead. We must lead because we have been created, chosen and called to do so. We must lead because we can hear the cries of our church and the call of our country to do so. We must lead because we can remain focused in the midst of chaos and withstand the fires of criticism. We must lead because we can overcome adversity to make a difference. We can lead because we are resilient and can get back up when we have been knocked down. We have the conscience, the compassion and the conviction to lead. We will be challenged on every hand but we will face that challenge and meet the demands thereof. We will do so because it is our choice to make what's happening in us supersede what happens to us. It is time for us, black women, to stand front and center and without delay or denial take the reins of leadership and make a difference in our schools, our churches, our communities, our courthouses, our country. And we must do so . . . because we can!

QUESTIONS FOR REFLECTION AND DISCUSSION

1. What are you willing to risk to lead?
2. In what areas of your life are you challenged most as it relates to your official or unofficial leadership?
3. What challenges are you willing to face so that you may lead?
4. How broad is your village?
5. Consider the needs of your community and how you might lend your talents and physical or monetary resources to its betterment.
6. What benefits could a Vision Day bring to your life and leadership? Reflect on ways that you might model this by example.

NOTES

Introduction: A Cry for Leadership
[1]Myles Munroe, *In Pursuit of Purpose* (Shippensburg, Penn.: Destiny Image, 1995), p. 8.
[2]Martin Luther King Jr., "Facing The Challenge of a New Age," in *A Testament of Hope: The Essential Writings of Martin Luther King, Jr.*, ed. James Melvin Washington (San Francisco: Harper & Row, 1986), p. 143.

Chapter 1: Being Chosen
[1]Felicia Griffin, "African-Americans Emerge as Market Giants with More Buying Power," *Houston Business Journal*, December 18, 1998 <http://houston.bizjournals.com/houston/stories/1998/12/21/smallb4>.
[2]"African American," *WOW!Facts 2001*, chap. 40, July 20, 2002 <www.ewowfacts.com/wowfacts/chapt40.html>.
[3]Jennifer Chambers, "Judge Refuses Mom's Guilty Plea," *Detroit News*, July 18, 2002 <http://detnews.com/2002/metro/0207/18/a01-540143/htm>.
[4]Commentary from *The NIV Study Bible* (Grand Rapids, Mich.: Zondervan, 1985), p. 1600.

Chapter 2: Responding to the Call
[1]"Philadelphia Girl Escapes from Kidnappers," *USA Today*, July 24, 2002 <www.usatoday.com/news/nation/2002-07-23-girl-found_x.htm>.
[2]Dennis P. Kimbro, *What Makes the Great Great* (New York: Doubleday, 1998), pp. 117-18.

Chapter 3: Facing Crisis
[1]From the POV/PBS documentary *Brother Outsider: The Life of Bayard Rustin*, prod. Nancy Kates, Bennett Singer and Sam Pollard, January 21, 2003. Additional information taken from Walter Naegle, "Bayard Rustin" <www.rustin.org/biography.html>.
[2]Spiros Zodhiates, *The Hebrew-Greek Key Study Bible* (Iowa Falls: World Bible Publishers, 1988), p. 1668.

Chapter 4: Acting with Courage
[1]"Harriet Ross Tubman," Microsoft Encarta Encyclopedia 2000.
[2]Dennis P. Kimbro, *What Makes the Great Great* (New York: Doubleday, 1998), p. 93.
[3]Mike Murdock, *The Assignment* (Tulsa, Okla.: Albury, 1997), p. 57.
[4]"Beverly Hannah: Architect Extraordinaire," April 1, 2003 <www.msu.edu/unit/msuaa/magazine/w96/hannah.htm>.

[5]"Fast-Food Queen Inspired by Faith," *Milwaukee Journal Sentinel,* March 29, 2003 <www.jsonline.com/news/metro/mar03/129673.asp>; Deborah Silver, "Urban Lure," *Restaurants and Institutions,* September 1, 2000 <www.rimag.com/017/Sr.htm>.

[6]Chris Goldman, "A Modern Day Deborah," *Pacific Church News,* Spring 1999, pp. 8-9.

Chapter 5: Listening to Your Conscience

[1]Mike Allen, "Bush Urges Crackdown on Business Corruption," *Washington Post,* July 9, 2002, p. A1.

[2]Prayer quoted by Martin Luther King Jr. in "Facing the Challenge of A New Age," in *A Testament of Hope: The Essential Writings of Martin Luther King, Jr.,* ed. James Melvin Washington (San Francisco: Harper & Row, 1986), p. 143.

[3]Bob Herbert, "Tobacco Dollars," *New York Times,* November 28, 1993, sect. 4, p. 11.

[4]David Ashenfelter, "Exec Is Convicted in Day-Care Fraud," *Detroit Free Press,* June 10, 1999, p. 2B.

[5]Jim Schaefer, "Detroiter's Excesses to Help Pay Debt," *Detroit Free Press,* November 22, 2000, p. 2A.

[6]W. E. B. Du Bois, *The Souls of Black Folk* (New York: Bantam, 1989), p. 57.

[7]"Pundit Pap for Sunday, April 26, 1998," *American Politics Journal* <www.american politics.com/042998PunditPap.html>.

Chapter 6: Maintaining Your Commitment

[1]David L. Evans, "Younger Generation of Blacks Soon Must Join Civil-Rights Fight," *Detroit Free Press,* February 26, 2002, p. 7A.

[2]Sylvia Rose, *Press On: Songs of Faith* (Detroit: Srose Publishing, 1985), p. 6.

Chapter 7: Developing Compassion

[1]"Charleszetta 'Mother' Waddles," Biography Resource Center, October 3, 2002 <www.africanpubs.com/Apps/bios/0099WaddlesCharleszetta.asp?pic=none>.

[2]John C. Maxwell, *The 21 Irrefutable Laws of Leadership* (Nashville: Thomas Nelson, 1998), p. 17.

[3]Julia A. Savacool, "The 2002 Heroes for Health Awards," *Family Health* <http://magazines.ivillage.com/goodhousekeeping/hb/health>; "Dr. Canady to Receive Athena Award," University of Michigan news release, June 13, 1995 <www.umich.edu/~newsinfo/Releases/1995/r061395a.html>.

[4]Laura Stojanovic, "2001's 10 Best Children's Hospitals: Doctors Who Make a Difference: Brain Breakthroughs," *Child,* February 2001 <www.child.com/kids/health_nutrition/top10_hospitals.jsp?page=7>.

[5]This story can be also be found in an article by James Walker, "Act of Kindness Speaks Volumes About Football's Spirit," *The Herald-Dispatch,* December 30, 2002

<www.wifca.org/pointaft/p99.html>.

[6]Patricia Sellers, "True Grit: The Most Powerful Women in Business," *Fortune* Online, September 27, 2002 <www.fortune.com/fortune/subs/article10,15114,370984,00.html>.

[7]Oprah Winfrey, interview, February 21, 1991, American Academy of Achievement online <www.achievement.org/autodoc/page/winOint-1>.

[8]Pam Farrel, *Woman of Influence* (Downers Grove, Ill.: InterVarsity Press, 1996), p. 8.

Chapter 8: Growing in Conviction

[1]Laurie Beth Jones, *Jesus, CEO* (New York: Hyperion, 1995), p. 51.

[2]"Mother Teresa," The Nobel Prize Internet Archive, October 15, 2002 <http://almaz.com/nobel/peace/1979a.html>.

[3]Rob Nagel, "Biography: Paul Robeson," *Contemporary Musicians* 8, September 1992, <www.homepage.sunrise.ch/homepage/comtex/rob3.htm>.

[4]David Willis, "Finding a Job Mentor Is a Must," *Detroit News,* March 12, 2003, p. 3B.

[5]BBC News, Americas, "Teen Editor Aims High," January 19, 2003 <http://news.bbc.co.uk/2/hi/americas/2668911.stm>.

[6]Cassandra Spratling, "The Heart of Black Poetry: Poets Are Coming to Detroit to Celebrate Naomi Long Madgett and 30 Years of Lotus Press," *Detroit Free Press,* October 8, 2002 <www.freep.com/entertainment/newsandreviews/lotus8_2002/008.htm>.

[7]David Willis, "Finding a Job Mentor Is a Must," *Detroit News,* March 12, 2003, p. 3B.

Chapter 9: Overcoming Challenges

[1]"HIV/AIDS Among African Americans," CDC-NCHSTP, Division of HIV/AIDS Prevention July 2003 <www.cdc.gov/hiv/pubs/facts/afam.htm>.

[2]Center for Disease Control and Prevention, "HIV/AIDS Among African Americans Key Facts: Cumulative Toll; Disease and Death," August 27, 2003 <www.cdc.gov.hiv/pubs/facts/afam.pdf>.

[3]Pamela Appea, "Bone Marrow Donation: More Blacks Need Apply," November 25, 2002 <www.Africana.com/DailyArticles/index_2>.